Praise for

A great read for anyone looking to figure out how to lead an organization and empower your teams.
– Gavriella Schuster | Corporate Vice President at Microsoft's One Commercial Partner Organization

I really enjoyed reading David's perspective and professional journey through sales. Giving real examples to back up his principles makes this an engaging read. I also love the fact that we treat sales as a profession that requires discipline and execution.
– Uttam Reddy | Senior VP Sales & Marketing at DoubleHorn

Why They Buy is a straightforward guide that shows you the art of getting your customer to sell themselves so that you don't have to! Study it and you'll become a master at understanding human behavior and your bottom line will benefit!
– Mark Nureddine | CEO, Bull Outdoor Products and bestselling author of *Pocket Mentor*

What a great perspective on complex, multi-level, B2B Selling! David's approach with the Fuess Method in *Why They Buy* really hits the mark. It's a comprehensive approach to building trust and delivering value while recognizing that when it comes to the final decision humans are still involved and if you haven't worked on the

emotional component of the sale you'll probably lose. His use of case studies and real life success stories add to the credibility of this sales approach. Highly recommended!
– Tom Fedro | President and CEO, Paragon Software Group Corporation

The Fuess Method is a highly effective blueprint to achieve successful results when navigating through the process of a complex sale. It is also much more than that. It applies to most aspects of running a successful business and perhaps, most importantly, it is also relevant to your personal life. The technique can be a game changer for sales, business and personal success. I thoroughly recommend reading it and adopting the method.
– Tony White | CEO and Founder, enChoice, Inc.

The approach presented in *Why They Buy* challenged my go-to sales approach and made me seriously reconsider how I should be trying to sell to potential customers. I enjoyed the book and really appreciated seeing some of what happened behind the scenes during Catapult's history! If you work in sales (and all of us realistically do whether we realize it or not), I would recommend checking this book out.
– Cameron Fuller | Solution Director for Launch at Catapult Systems

This concise and straight-to-the-point guide will show you how the art of the sale creates customers for life. It's invaluable to anyone who wants to influence behavior not only in the sales industry, but in personal relationships, or managing a team of employees. I highly recommend this book not only to salespeople but also to anyone who is interested in the topic.

– Ali Razi | Founder and CEO, Banc Certified Merchant Services

As a young business professional, this book was a monumental learning experience for my career. Whether it's in our job title or not, sales is involved in our daily lives all of the time. Not only does David Fuess touch this concept, but his sales methodology is something I plan on using for the rest of my business career going forward.

– Trent Warren | Social Media and Engagement Specialist at DoubleHorn

'Sell trust, not a product or service.' Truer sales words have never been written! David's innate ability to get to the core of what people don't even know they need is exceptional.

– Aynsley Interiano | Principal and Event Planning Consultant at RedWave Consulting

Why They Buy is about planting seeds in the minds of prospective customers so that they can ponder how their needs are satisfied by buying your product or service. The author's assumption is that people want to be led to a solution by providing some 'handholding' and letting people come to their own conclusions. The book is well written and provides unconventional selling advice.

– Dr Joseph S. Maresca | CPA, CISA

Why They Buy will become the successful salesman's handbook; the cornerstone for knowing how to ask the right, carefully thought-out questions to gain confident commitment from others. The Fuess Method is a powerful tool for leadership with far-reaching applications for creating consensus in business, in the community, and in the family. Filled with great examples of how to influence an individual's thought process and inspire team work, *Why They Buy* is a must-read for all business management universities.

– Elaine D. Brazzell | Professor, Northwood University

I found David Fuess to be a master in the art of selling. *Why They Buy* is a resourceful book for those who want to sell, but also for leaders. To be an effective leader, you need to get your followers to... follow. The Fuess Method gives an example of how you can do this. I love the concept of letting your customer talk themselves into needing your product. I found the art of David Fuess's success can be applied to all relationships and is key to making you successful in many areas.

– Readers' Favorite, five stars

Leaders
Press

WHY THEY BUY

A Bulletproof Method to Closing Any Sale

by
David Fuess
with Apollo Gonzalez

Leaders
Press

Leaders
Press

ISBN 978-1-943386-32-1 (pbk)

ISBN 978-1-943386-31-4 (ebook)

Library of Congress Control Number: 2018964036

This book is dedicated to the profession of sales.

Yes, I said profession. It's amazing that this craft is still not taught in our school systems today. Most people have a negative perception of salespeople, yet without these folks there would be no revenue, no customers, and *no business*! We can all continually refine our approach to selling and improve the misperceptions. There are good ones and bad ones just like any other profession. With this book, I hope to create more of the former or at least fewer of the latter.

FREE BOOKLET!

Are you ready to realize the full potential of digitization in your business?

Ready to get more done, enhance your company culture, support your employees' productivity, and ensure your customers' data is safe and secure?

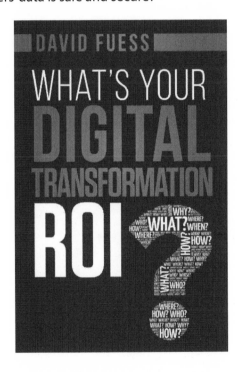

Go to https://get.catapultsystems.com/freebie/ and download a free copy of *What's Your Digital Transformation ROI?* to discover the digital transformation your business is missing.

CONTENTS

MEET DAVID FUESS

"I just got Fuessed again!"

I only realized that my former business partner David Fuess had a unique way of doing things the day I said to him, "I just got Fuessed again!" When he asked what I was talking about, I said that the way he went about selling ideas was that it was always my own idea that I bought.

"I always buy into what you're selling because it's my own idea. Months later, I realize that it wasn't my idea at all; I just came to your conclusion," I said, laughing.

At that time, I could see that David hadn't considered that he did things differently from other sales people. He asked me if I thought his method was a little deceitful or slick.

"No way!" I assured him.

His method isn't at all deceptive or tricky. It's merely a common-sense way of helping others see something that he already knows, and then allowing them to sell themselves on their own ideas.

As the CEO of Catapult Systems, David doesn't get the chance to sell face to face as often as he used to. Catapult now has a sales force, a sales management team and a senior management team. But David's still selling every day. He's selling ideas and concepts to the Catapult employees, who in turn sell them to the customers.

Sales, as David often says, is a never-ending cycle of opportunities.

To be successful, he must have a clear vision of what he ultimately wants to sell to his constituencies, and he has to think through the tactics to sell them. Within that context, it's rare today that an idea he wants to sell is not sold. When David is in front of a customer, it's unlikely that they won't buy unless they have no needs, in which case they wouldn't be sitting together in the first place. His hit rate is quite high, and it's not because he's the most charming guy; it's his learned ability to ask the right questions, and to listen to the answers.

Having worked with David so closely for several years, it dawned on me that many of the various agenda items or decisions that we moved forward with at Catapult weren't my ideas, but his. Over time, with his approach — and after experiencing his process over a few years — I realized that the ideas or initiatives didn't necessarily originate with me.

While I was the one who put the solution on the table, David had been driving the agenda or initiative all along through his question-and-answer method. I'd just been led to the process, and to the set of conclusions and initiatives that made it seem like it was my idea.

The Fuess Method (as it's come to be informally known) is a way of planting the seed of an idea in your mind through a series of questions that lead you to a logical outcome — and one that you wouldn't propose if you didn't think it was a good idea anyway. It's a unique way of having you take the credit for making your own decision.

Early on, David recognized that the single most valuable thing he could do, given his background, was to help his salespeople and support staff refine their craft. He now does a lot of sales teaching, as he's an expert at Fuessing. Catapult Systems has grown quite a bit over the years, and the company now has a sales force of about 30 people.

Seeing that David sells in a different way that results in success, I suggested that he teach others how to do it. I urged him to share his knowledge. The book you now hold in your hands will walk you down the path of understanding how, using the Fuess Method, you will sell customers on their own ideas.

Catapult's projects as case studies

Using Catapult case studies throughout the book will allow you to see how Catapult's sales team sells complicated solutions to customers in real time using the Fuess Method. The vision and foresight they use on a daily basis helps customers to transform digitally so they don't get left behind. Catapult's digital suite of solutions is proven to accomplish this goal, and the examples in the book all apply.

The Fuess Method's insight into selling is genuine, and David's approach is very educational, allowing business decision-makers and/or sales professionals to pivot and clearly see the business outcomes they're hoping to achieve. Regardless of your industry, you'll see through any fog in your industry that has been caused by the ever-changing technology world.

The Fuess Method has been applied in everything that David's done, but that's just the framework that supports Catapult's success. In reading *Why They Buy*, business leaders and salespeople will be educated and enlightened through reading the specific case studies. In exploring Catapult's solutions and how they're sold, you'll see how David combines passion and an ability to channel his energy into a model which people rally around to drive vision and clarity.

The *art* of the sale is one of the essential key differences in this book.

As I'm sure you know, there's an impressive landscape of smart and proven sales tactics that have already been developed, ranging from Dale Carnegie's 1936 publication *How to Win Friends and Influence People* to a whole host of subsequent and different methodologies. A couple of them are discussed in the next chapter.

David often says he gives a lot of kudos to the creators of these foundational texts. This book isn't intended to replace those popular methodologies, but to dovetail nicely right in with them. See, this book is different from other sales tactics and "how to influence people" books. The science these other sales giants have taught is the technique, and that, of course, is important. No one will argue with that, as salespeople need to understand the techniques behind successful selling. The earlier, popular sales techniques are primarily scientific, though. This book will teach you the *art* of the sale.

There's a lot behind selling methodologies. The science side is the easy part of learning, by the way. Learning science is much easier than learning an art, as art is, by definition, subjective. Every single situation that a salesperson will face throughout her career is going to be different, and her art has to adjust to each unique situation. But the science of the case may be similar, if not exactly the same, across the board.

Sales is an art form that requires an understanding of human nature + motivation.

Certainly, some artists are born artistic — no question about it. The good news is that art can be taught, and even a natural-born artist can become better through learning. This book will meet you where you are in your sales journey. You'll learn to flex new artistic muscles that will make you much more well-rounded in your dealings with other people, both personally and professionally.

The real art of sales lies in the understanding that every single person we deal with in the world is different. Given that, how do we use one sales method on them all that works across the board? Despite their inherent differences, the one thing that people have in common is that they all have the ability to sell themselves on an idea or concept. As you will learn, what is key to this sales method is that every single human on this planet is capable of selling themselves.

We're all selling something — ourselves, our ideas, our points of view, our products or our services — and the concept of business is basically creating relationships so we can sell. Being able to influence people is important. You want them to buy from you. You want to develop a relationship. Businesses sell ideas, concepts, products and services but ultimately — and this is very important — it's human beings and not companies that buy, so it's vitally important to be good at influencing people.

The Fuess Method of selling is smart and straightforward; a unique way of selling a concept by asking a series of questions and relying on the customer's own intelligence to sell themselves on the idea. That talky, aggressive persona telling you what to think and how to think it and how buying their product will cure all your ills is outdated. With the advent of the Internet, today's customers are more intelligent, savvy and rational than ever before.

The real art of sales lies in getting people to buy their own ideas from themselves.

This method of sales you're going to learn is something that you'll find applicable throughout your entire life, not just in the business realm. Even if you think you can't see a way to apply this method to your business, keep reading, because in any relationship you can use the Fuess Method effectively to get what you want.

The reason the Fuess Method is effective is that you don't have to do much other than create the environment for your customer to buy his own idea. That's really a double bonus, because one, you've sold something, and two, your customer becomes incredibly invested in what you sold because it's his very own idea.

The second part of this equation is essential: every day your customer has a choice whether they will continue to consume or buy your product or service or idea. Every single day they can make a decision to remain on board or change their choice. Naturally, you can't be there all the time.

But guess who's in front of your customer all the time. They are. If you've helped them get to the point where they love what they came up with, you don't need to be there every day. Instead, they get to convince themselves every day how great a decision it was to buy from you.

By learning this method, you'll learn how to capitalize on the opportunity to be the best in your space at selling in a new way to your constituents or stakeholders, whether they be employees or customers. You'll learn how to apply some critical psychological concepts to this new and different premise that you've never heard of before.

In today's world, we need to be able to conduct business without getting to know each other in person.

This is very important. Not all purchase decisions are necessarily based on relationships (as was the case in the past), but relationships do influence a large part of the equation. They're simply approached differently in today's world. If we don't have a direct one-on-one relationship and you want me to buy your product or my service, I need to be able to do so without meeting you. In fact, that's where the digital component of conducting business without a relationship becomes very important.

To be successful in our endeavors, we need to be able to influence people to retain our services or buy our products in the digital world. If you don't have the time or the platform to get to know your potential customers in a personal way, the Fuess Method can be applied to a more general level. Fundamentally, if it's their idea, the likelihood that they're going to buy it goes up dramatically.

Most importantly, the method you are going to learn isn't tricky, nor is it deceitful.

It's recognizing that your potential customer has a need for what you can provide. When you follow through on this recognition by asking questions, your customers will tell you what it is they need. When you use the Fuess Method, your customers will walk themselves right into buying your product or service because they realize they need it. That's the magic behind the Fuess Method.

By turning the table and asking your customer specific questions, they come up with the right answer (which was, by the way, the answer you had in the first place). You ask the right questions, but your customer falls in love with the idea because it's theirs.

You never take credit for it, either. You can utilize this method in a non-digital way, and you can also do it digitally. The process has to be quite subtle to work, and then when they come up with the *eureka* idea, they think, "Yes! Perfect! It's exactly what I wanted. What a great decision I've made!"

Sam Goodner
Founder of Catapult Systems

Let's dive a little deeper by first acknowledging some great books that you can read to round out your sales education and combine with the Fuess Method. Dale Carnegie's *How to Win Friends and Influence People* is such a useful book for people in sales to read. Some 80 years after publication, the advice about keeping it positive, and gearing conversation around asking questions of the other party are quite relevant. After all, making an excellent first impression, finding good ways to criticize people, and learning tricks for being better at conversation never go out of style.

There are other classics, such as *Strategic Selling and Conceptual Selling* by Stephen E. Heiman and Robert B. Miller, as well as Mahan Khalsa's *Let's Get Real or Let's Not Play*. Another classic is Neil Rackham's *SPIN Selling*. Those books immediately come to mind when thinking of the classics, as they illustrate the primary sales methods or philosophies out there. None of these popular sales bibles teach the approach that I'm going to talk about. As I've mentioned, these books teach the science of selling, while the Fuess Method teaches the art of selling.

A newer book out on the market is called *The Challenger Sale* by Matthew Dixon and Brent Adamson. It's garnered a lot of popularity, and it's also great science. The challenger sale is probably the most credible selling methodology on the market today. But it's missing something. While the authors present a fantastic selling methodology, they don't discuss the art of the sale. That's where the Fuess Method comes in.

Art can complement popular science methodology.

Traditionally, most sales are considered to be relation-ship-oriented. By nature, a relationship takes time to develop. It's soft. It's intangible. It involves a significant amount of human-to-human face time or conversation time to build trust, to build confidence, to build a relationship. The exciting thing about a challenger sale is that it tries to break through that stereotype or concept that sales is a relationship-oriented thing that takes a lot of time to develop. Instead, it says, "No. If I've got a mouse trap and it's a game changer, and it's disruptive, you should buy it whether you like me or not."

It's true to some degree that people buy from people they like, and that's certainly important. But the challenger sale presents a way to go right to the core faster to learn what a buyer is looking for and to be more challenging about it. You're not there just to be a soft relationship builder. You go in there and ask the hard questions, and even be a little bit confrontational. But the method relies on having a unique and disruptive widget to sell.

For example, you might sell a Tesla doing the challenger sale, but you're probably not going to sell a classic sedan when there are tons of sedans out there to choose from. The Tesla differs radically from everything else on the market, so you can be very bold with it, and the challenger sale relies on having something very bold to sell.

Say you're gung-ho on the challenger type of sale, and that's the scientific methodology you're committed to. Now imagine adding my artistic method to the deal; adding another layer to your tactics. You can easily take your disruptive product and skip the relationship-building part, yet add in all the right questions that lead your prospect down the path to purchase. Combining the two tactics would work organically well.

Examine the influences within an organization and understand how they react to each other.

SPIN Selling by Neil Rackham is a classic, and all the big companies, such as the Xeroxes and the Kodaks, have educated their sales forces in SPIN selling. There's also *The New Conceptual Selling* and *The New Strategic Selling*, both written by Robert Miller and Stephen Heiman. *The Trusted Advisor* by David H. Maister, Charles H. Green and Robert M. Galford is another important classic.

These books each offer an in-depth look at the various buying influences within an organization and an understanding of how they interrelate with each other, and how to communicate effectively with each of those buying influences within an enterprise or an account. They bring to life the personas involved with the buy side so that as a seller — and as a selling site — you understand all the roles of the people involved and the implications of what their part is in the sale. In *The Trusted Advisor*, the authors argue that the key to professional success is the ability to earn the trust and confidence of clients.

The Fuess Method has taken all of those concepts and materials and layered them into a new artful method of selling. What we talk about in this book is something that's not covered in any of those other scientific books. Together, however, science and art are valuable. You can get those foundational methodologies down and refine your craft. It would be difficult to be very successful with the method we're suggesting without an understanding of some of the foundational elements from one or all of those books. You do have to understand the science behind the methods.

Telling stories is a very artful way of creating an environment or setting the mood for you to begin selling a particular idea or a concept.

A classic around storytelling is *Managing by Storying Around* by David Armstrong. This book covers the art of telling stories as psychology, as does *The Art of Storytelling* by Nancy Mellon. These books were invaluable at a point in time when storytelling was being incorporated into the Fuess Method. The reason storytelling is so valuable and is an essential aspect of our method is that telling stories differs significantly from selling something, but not if you do it very artfully. You can do both at the same time, and it looks like you aren't trying to sell something when you tell stories.

What underscores the power of storytelling is the concept of how you can influence others through mind pictures. If we're telling a story, it's going to be told in a very artful way. It's conjuring up specific thoughts, certain pictures, and images in your mind. When it's done artfully, those pictures can do the selling for you, because there's something attractive about that picture, image, smell or whatever it might be that's attractive. We've helped put you in that spot through telling a story. We have to know what idea or concept we're selling, of course, before we start storytelling.

That's where the art comes in. You want to learn how someone absorbs information as quickly as possible. Say you've only known someone for an hour and a half and they seem very analytical. They don't seem to have a super high or a super low temperament. If you were going to tell a story, you wouldn't want to choose a hyped-up story or a tragic story; you would try to appeal to the thinking nature. The art of telling a story is quickly picking up cues from the other person, and then creating an environment through a story you believe they might respond to. Storytelling is a method of psychology in selling, and it certainly is tied into our method.

Psychology and leadership are useful for teaching sales skills and inspiring sales methodology.

My mother was a psychologist, and so I grew up in an environment of understanding how people respond situationally, why they react in certain ways, and the underlying psychology of being a human being. The art of my method takes into account a lot of psychology. The other concept I read a lot about and I take courses in is leadership. Any time I can, I take a new course on leadership as I believe inspiration is derived from leadership. I find topics around what motivates people kind of fascinating such as fear, carrot-and-stick concepts and why people respond in certain ways to certain situations.

The Fuess Method takes psychology and leadership into account. Some people read leadership books to learn how to move up the food chain of a company, for example. That's probably one of the more common reasons for reading books on leadership. They seek to learn how to appeal to people in a particular way. The more exciting part is determining which traits allow them to influence and inspire the people around them.

By the way, if you're selling digitally, then by nature, you're already leading. You may lead unsuccessfully, or you may lead successfully, but if you are seeking to influence and inspire someone on a digital platform, you're leading, as that's a significant form of leadership. Whether it has a leadership title or not isn't as important as the act itself.

People want to be led. Even the most influential people in the world still like to be led, and they typically find guidance from the spiritual side. When you apply that to the business side, CEOs want to be led, but they're also leading. You can do it with sticks or carrots, and both can be effective, and in fact, at different times, perhaps both need to be used.

The best kind of leadership is inspirational, as it helps the people you're leading become better than they thought they could ever be.

Leading through inspiration helps those around you find that extra 20 percent or that sixth gear or whatever you want to call it. They do it willingly, excitingly and enthusiastically. Inspirational leadership helps you get the best out of your people. We apply the same ideas to leadership by leading without doing it overtly. For example, Catapult Systems doesn't do just one job. We fulfill many roles for customers so we can get incredibly creative with how we present our solutions to a customer, how a customer buys them, or what they do with them.

We offer a palette of tools, so it's a matter of arranging the colors and the textures in ways that ensure the customer doesn't feel sold to but instead thinks that it's their idea to choose instead of ours. In many regards, buying truly is their idea. It's not like we're magicians and pull doves from our hats. We want you to figure out that you stuck the dove in the hat. We're invested in the psychology of you creating your need, and you creating your solution. We just help you. We inspire you. We help you to formulate it. And by doing so, we both succeed. The way we accomplish this is through leadership.

The number of people we all touch is almost endless. If you're a human being, then you're being led, and you're leading other people throughout your day — whether it's your family or your friends or your colleagues. The application of what we're talking about applies across someone's life from start to finish in almost any regard, as opposed to being just about selling in a corporate environment.

People who sell successfully year after year tend to have a system.

Another book to mention is *Creating Rainmakers* by Ford Harding. A rainmaker in a business sense is someone who year after year produces impressive results. The author goes inside the mind of rainmakers to figure out what magic they have that leads them to generate rain — or big sales — year after year. The author did find some commonalities. While each of the concepts is important, one of them is around creating value with ideas which are very similar to storytelling.

There are similar scientific elements around how rainmakers target their customer, and how they prospect, as well as the other fundamental aspects of successful salespeople. They create systems for themselves, and naturally, the systems vary from rainmaker to rainmaker, but they each create a system that works for them.

The book discusses the importance of being a good listener and sympathizer as a rainmaker. That concept is a fundamental concept of the Fuess Method as well. The book also discusses the finessing of a sale. Another way of saying that is that creativity, or the art form, is crucial.

Where that ties into the method is that we don't come into a meeting with one thing in mind that we want to convince a potential customer to do. That's never the intention.

We know there are many things a customer could possibly do. Because they're a target prospect of ours, and we know they're a likely prospect — they would consume the type of services we offer — then it's our job to provide the creativity element. They may by nature be far more creative than we are. In this situation, we have to get their creative juices to turn on, and we have to be creative in getting them to think about potential solutions, so finessing is about creativity.

THE FUESS METHOD

The Fuess Method: an egoless sales method whereby the agent leads the customer to believe that the idea originated with and belongs to the customer

The primary elements of the Fuess Method are:

First	You help your customer establish their why.
Second	Your customer believes that you are on their ride.
Third	You engage your customers with a series of questions.
Fourth	Your customer arrives at an idea that you've led them to through your series of questions.
Fifth	You don't take the credit; the customer takes the credit for their idea.

MY STORY

In high school and college, I used to wait tables — an excellent job for any young person to learn how to communicate, recognize the eccentricities of customers and still try to make them happy. When I graduated from college, I had no idea what I wanted to do. I thought I would play professional football, but that didn't pan out. I thought I'd be a lawyer and then decided not to go to law school. I got a few decent job offers after college, and one of them happened to be in sales.

I didn't think highly of the sales profession at the time, but I thought, "I'm very competitive, and sales is very competitive, and if I'm competing against other people every day, my natural juices will kick in, and I know I can be successful." I had to learn everything from scratch as I had no idea how to sell anything; not an idea, a concept, a product or a service. I was just a kid who went through college, and they don't teach you anything about sales in college.

I hit the road. I went out and started selling. I knew I needed to learn, so I took different courses and training, and I learned methodologies, such as consultative and strategic selling. I learned the science behind identifying different kinds of buyers. Gradually, I designed a process that I felt was a better method for me, building upon all of the learning I've mentioned in the previous chapter, such as Miller and Heiman and the challenger sale. I included those vital scientific elements in my method.

One thing I learned along the way was that I needed to be selling to smart people. They were my audience because they're typically the ones with the money and the companies. Once I identified that they were my audience, I drilled down into discovering their characteristics and how to sell to them. Given the method, it's time to explore the key sales characteristics behind a successful Fuesser.

KEY SALES CHARACTERISTICS OF THE FUESS METHOD

Ask the big question: Why?

In the Fuess Method, as part of helping customers develop their idea, a critical part of our role is first to help drive clarity in their mental picture and vision of the end state. We help them examine their why. This may look like dissatisfaction with the status quo, the desire to have the latest and greatest, or the need to be an early adopter. Assisting customers with exploring, defining, and acknowledging their reasons for seeking transformation puts you in the catbird seat.

Let's say we're meeting with a company that we have already deemed is a target customer. We've done our due diligence, and so we have established that the customer could use our solutions as a service. Early in the Fuess Method, we establish their need for change and the why for their change. As a part of helping our customer develop their idea, a key part of our method is to help them paint a picture of what our solution will look like once it's already established in their company. Once the why is established, customers become open to solving their problem.

With Catapult customers, for example, their why to buy may be because they have an employee satisfaction or engagement issue with their employees on their intranet. If their employees aren't fully engaged, they're not getting a lot of excitement or productivity or loyalty. That's a big why we often face when selling to our customers. We look at that and agree that's a big problem, as employee disruption with engagement can stifle and disrupt the business.

These answers are all entirely predictable. We already know everything we're going to hear. Rather than come in and say, "Hey, let me show you Fuse," we're coming in, and we're Fuessing them, which is to start with, "Tell me your sandbox of pain." They want to share their sandbox because it's been painful for them for so long. Then we start moving them through the process a question at a time as to how Fuse will benefit their employees.

There has to be a reason for a change, a reason for movement, a reason for buying an idea, concept, product or service. When we go to the customer, we approach them differently and say, "What if we were to give you an intranet for free and you never had to repurchase one? It would always have the latest technology, and instead of paying for the intranet, you pay us on a monthly basis to keep the content fresh for your employees." We help them come up with the idea why they would decide to drop a single intranet purchase method and switch to our monthly solution as a service. This is where the art comes in. This is when we happen to be conveniently sitting on the other side of the desk, or behind the computer screen, ready to sell what will solve their problems.

Sell higher level ideas to people when they see a need to purchase from you and invite you on their ride.

Now, if smart people are skeptical by nature, that means you're going to have difficulty selling your idea to them. At the very least, they're going to be slow to accept it, most likely because it wasn't their idea to begin with. They will be most likely to accept what they came up with because they tricked themselves into thinking they're the smartest people that they know. We pander to those people who subscribe to that way of thinking, and we developed the Fuess Method around working with the common-denominator qualities of the people we're selling ideas and concepts to.

We have sold to very intelligent buyers. We've been fortunate to have engineers of all sorts as our customer base, whether they're software engineers or mechanical engineers, and they're some of the hardest people on the planet to sell to. That probably helped us refine how we were selling better than anything else.

There's a saying that some of the hardest people to convince that God exists are the most intelligent people. The reason why is because they're used to having all the answers. When you can get behind that and acknowledge that you're used to having the answers, we're going to let you do that. We're going to let you come up with the solution all by yourself, except you're going to come up with the answer we wanted you to come up with; you just don't know it yet. That's why the method is so powerful.

If you decide you want to buy a house or a car, you first have to have the idea that you would like a new one, or that you need a new one. So our first job is to sell you the concept that a new car would be a good idea for you, and this is where the digital component comes into view. Digitally, we connect concepts to people, both internally, meaning employees, or externally, meaning paying customers.

This is an ask-and-listen approach; it's not a tell approach.

Early in my sales career, my sales managers would tell me, "You see the answer or solution to things very quickly, but you get in too big of a hurry getting the other party to your answer and move on. That's frustrating for both parties." Even if my idea happened to be the right one for the prospect, I was met with resistance due to my speed, fervor and persistence. I needed a new approach!

I realized I needed to flip it completely around — move at their pace and have it be their answer. The trick was having their answer be the right answer or solution. I also had to learn how to funnel the prospect to the right answer while making it their idea at the same time. That's key!

Salespeople can be known to feature-and-benefit you to death — or at least until you purchase. They corner you and circle you and try to talk you into something they want you to do. For example, if you go to a car lot, the person selling you a car follows a rudimentary methodology that he has been taught. They walk you down the path, and if you know it for what it is, you'll quickly recognize it. It's a relatively simple series of questions. The first question is always, "So how much of a monthly payment do you want?" That question is generally followed by, "Do you like fast cars?" and then, "Do you have a big family?" The salesperson will ask fundamental questions to get you into a car that very day.

Most intelligent people are quite skeptical by nature. Yet, generally speaking, the smarter you are, the more likely you are to fall in love with your own ideas. You're accustomed to having better ideas than your neighbors, whether that was in school, the business world or at home. You're likely to have become accustomed to having the brightest idea in the room or at least what you think is the most brilliant idea in the room.

You'll become more effective in meetings when you realize that listening to your customer talk is a whole lot more effective than talking. Why? Because people like to hear themselves talk more than they like to hear you talk. That applies to just about everybody; they like their ideas better than yours.

The Fuess Method talks nobody into anything; you talk yourself into it. Our job is to help you understand what you want and then have you recognize that we are offering a solution to that problem. You don't feel like you're being sold to when we allow you to come up with your own solution via the ask-and-listen approach.

Sell trust, not a product or a s

Your customers are buying the
They're buying a vision; squishy
get your arms around. Let's say y
and you want the customer to go a
you. Begin by working backward. You
it that you feel like the idea is a goo
for you. Once you understand why it's   ., you
go through the steps of allowing them t   ..n their own
conclusion that the concept is a great one.

Rather than pointing out the steps that will lead them to that conclusion, ask a series of questions. Start with some common denominator, and perhaps some simple setup questions without it seeming like a setup — because then it doesn't work. You come into the situation already knowing the outcome you want.

The reason why Sam Goodner spoke of getting Fuessed is that Sam loves Sam's ideas, just as most people love their own ideas. The success rate of getting him to do or move or act on something was so high that over time, he was able to reflect and ruminate and figure out what was going on. It took Sam five years to figure out what was happening when he was Fuessed, so this method isn't some elementary process where you experience it once and feel like you were duped and never want to do it again. Quite the opposite, this method helps people come to a conclusion that it's good for them.

Become skilled at listening and asking questions, and watch how the perception of the person on the other side of the table improves.

The art of listening is one of the more difficult things for earn. People speak naturally. Typically, while ⟨on⟩e is talking, the other person is trying to figure ⟨out⟩ what they're going to say next, as opposed to genuinely listening. The skill of listening involves practice, pain, energy and effort. There are specific techniques that people can practice to learn to listen. One is to decide for the whole day, or even just for an hour, that for every statement you make, you're going to ask four questions. You start to realize how often you're telling and speaking versus inquiring. That mode of inquiry is going to require you to listen, and listening takes energy.

Furthermore, for every time that someone else makes a statement, you ask at least one, and preferably two questions to clarify what you heard. Practice that. It's not easy. The interaction becomes so much better for your customer as a result of them feeling like they were actually heard. The whole concept around listening and asking the right questions is fundamental to the Fuess Method. In fact, it's a requirement to be effective at this method.

Say you set the goal that for any time someone makes a statement, you are going to ask a clarifying question to make sure you understand what they said. Your customer could mean five different things, and you might think they meant one thing when it could have been four other things. If you ask a clarifying question, to do that in the first place, you have to be listening. Otherwise, you're going to ask some left-field question, which would have the opposite effect you are hoping to have.

Be fully present and in the moment to clarify what the person is saying.

The other thing skilled listening will force you to do is become good at asking clarifying questions without being annoying or offensive. Offensiveness can be because of tone, the words you use or your body language. But if you're in the moment and you're trying hard to clarify what someone is saying, you become quite skillful at asking these questions in different ways in which it doesn't look canned, and it's not annoying and offensive. It's achievable, but it takes practice.

There are a lot of techniques for asking questions that don't sound offensive. One we employ often is "So, I think I know what you meant when you said that, but I just want to make sure. Would you mind restating what you said just so that I'm clear?" You've just said to them, "Hey, I'm listening to you, and now I'm listening even more closely." What will happen is that they'll say it a second time in a slightly different manner than they did the first time, which clarifies what they were saying.

Another way to say it is "What you just said elicits several different thoughts in my mind. But before I go off on a tangent on one of those thoughts, would you mind clarifying what you meant? I heard the words, but I want to understand the meaning behind them." That's another way of telling someone, "Hey, I'm listening to you. I'm listening carefully. I don't want any misunderstandings between us, so let me hear it again."

You might think that would be annoying, but you'd be surprised that it's not. When someone asks you those questions, your response most likely is going to be along the lines of "Wow, they are really listening to me, and they are listening carefully to me. They are asking me to clarify what I just said, and people don't normally do that. They care about my answers; they care about me."

Sometimes, when you really get people going, they start vomiting words out in saying what they're thinking. But if you ask a clarifying question, it helps the speaker to shift his thoughts and become more dialed into what he's saying. Being connected to the conversation is a perfect term to describe this interaction. Another way of saying it is that it warms the room, creating a warmer atmosphere, one where we're going to communicate on a more intimate level. We're not going to surf along the surface of a conversation, which is where most people live in their communications and relationships.

As leaders and sellers of ideas or concepts, our objective is to go deeper. These different techniques allow you to get below the surface without becoming obtrusive or annoying unless that person is ready and willing to go there. If they want to go there and share, great. You're going to create an even deeper connection with them. If they don't want to, that's fine too. But your approach is warming the environment to allow for that to happen.

Become very attuned to the people that you're selling to.

Learn to hear what's said and what's not said. Hear why it was said or not said, because you have to become that good at it. If your method to sell is going to be asking questions rather than telling someone what you think they should do, then you must become very good at understanding answers and framing up situations. As long as somebody has a need — and let's assume everybody you talk to has a need — your hit rate should be quite high.

In the Fuess Method, you'll learn to remove the words 'I' and 'me' from your vocabulary. It can't be about me anymore. If I'm selling you on your idea, then it has to be about you. I must make myself irrelevant in these scenarios as the seller of the concept, as the more irrelevant I am, the more important you become, and the more likely you are to act on what you perceive to be your idea.

The phrase to repeat mentally is "I'm here for your ride." The more you can get into that mindset, the more successful this method will be. What you find is that as you start seeing this method work, and then work again and again, you realize that the whole 'I' concept can take a backseat. It's not necessary anymore, and you find yourself using it less in your life. People who know me think I'm one of the most humble people that they know. The truth of the matter is I like myself as much as the next person likes themselves, but they think I'm humble because I don't speak in the first person anymore.

For an online sale, you're not going to be standing in front of your potential customers, so you need to know the right questions to ask in the digital realm — as well as how to ask them. You have to know your audience and what's important to them. You have to have a tailored solution that will fit your audience's need; something that you can provide; something they need or want.

Certain people are targets for your solutions or services, and certain people are not. You don't want to sell to someone who's not a good target, so you do have to entice the right people to interact with you. You have to slice and dice the demographics and do target marketing. If you're bringing the right audience to the table, there's a very high likelihood that they have a need for something you provide.

Use a funneling technique of asking questions to lead your customer gracefully to your answer.

You use this technique because you go into sales scenarios with a solution that you already believe is good for the customer. You would like to get them to that answer. At the top of the funnel, you ask the big generic questions, not the yes/no questions. They're open-ended questions at the top, and as you get down to the bottom of the funnel, the yes/no questions help you refine what you've already begun putting together.

If you walk in and say to your potential customer, "This is the answer", they will resist it. They meet the same criteria or characteristics of other smart people, and they don't like to be sold to. They don't want to do it, just because it was your idea and not theirs. One of our natural instincts is to resist when we feel like we're being sold to. If you think it was my idea, you're going to resist. You might think, "Gosh, I should've thought of that" and you're, therefore, going to resist that idea just because you can. The idea has to come first, and it has to be your idea. Asking the right questions in the proper format funnels them into a place that has a good outcome for both of you — using your questions and their ideas.

Once you get to the bottom of the funnel, then you can brainstorm, and the answer you come up with will be a win because it's something that you can help them with. The magic part is when you get to "The options are A, B and C. Which one do you like the best?" They came up with A, B and C (or at least they think they did), but you massaged them there on the way without them feeling manipulated. They now get to select which one they want. Your company made A, B and C, so you're both benefiting, and they get exactly what you wanted.

Use this method at a pace with which your customer is comfortable.

Different people get sold at different paces. Some people are very methodical and like to analyze until they're ready to make a decision. Other people want to make a decision very rapidly. It's about them, not about you, and the more it's about them, the more likely it is that the sale of the idea or concept will take place. You have to take them through this process of allowing them to do what they do naturally, which is to fall in love with their own ideas. You can help them fall in love with their own ideas as fast as they want to go.

Most salespeople talk too much and miss the opportunity to let the person that is being sold to do the talking, which is ultimately doing the selling. People love to hear themselves speak, which is a good thing for the person who's selling to them. Ideally, if you're asking the right questions, you will get them talking, and they will talk themselves into a solution, and that solution will be the one that you had already decided was the right one in the first place.

Your job is to figure out how to get their ideas out of them, and once you do that, you have them in a situation where they're ready to marry up with what you're offering. Put the why questions out there, such as why it's important to them. Once they convince themselves — which is the magic behind the whole method — that this is a big enough pain for them, then they conclude to buy all by themselves. At that point, you are conveniently sitting right in front of them, and that's precisely what you can help them with.

Break your customer free from natural resistances.

At Catapult Systems, after we sell trust, we sell not a product but a service — custom software development. This is an important distinction because we needed a sales method that didn't yet exist to sell the service. Our services-as-a-solutions model didn't have features and benefits, so it was squishy, and we had to give it life during our sales presentations. We had to give people a reason to buy our service, so it was one of the hardest things you could sell.

A service is hard to define because it's not a service in a box; it's defined, designed, and based on the individual customer's needs. It had a different answer for every customer because each had a need that we aimed to solve through custom development. We could make software do virtually anything if we defined the need well enough, so through the process of selling something as tricky as it was to sell, we tried all the methods in all the books and everything we had been trained on and still fell short. There was too much art in what we were selling for those methods to work on their own.

There first has to be a need for what your product does. Then the question becomes one of how to sell the idea that the customer needs your product. If you can sell him on the idea — which was his idea, and not yours — you're then in the catbird seat to have your product beat any competitors because he'll feel a unique sense of appreciation towards you for helping him come up with his idea.

Inspire movement in a direction you want him to move in so you cannot be manipulative or malicious.

This method is built upon the idea that you're both honest people who want the best for each other. You can't feel you've been manipulated into something that you're going to be upset about later. The reason why Sam Goodner laughs now about getting Fuessed is that he knew that any decision he made was because it was the right decision for him. If you realize your idea isn't the right one for your customer, you have to be willing to disengage.

What it comes down to is how much does the customer trust you. As salespeople wanting to provide a service, we've got only so much time to sell to you. When you're making a final decision, you're going to make it based on how much you enjoyed talking to me or how much you trusted our face. That's the reality of it, as much as you don't want to admit these sorts of things.

"It's hard to see what's happening when the method is used on you infrequently," Sam says. "If you're going through this method as the recipient of it and it's your first time or second time, and the other person is good at it, it's hard to recognize what's going on. It took me a while with David, and I was working closely with him. He does it just naturally. It's just the way he communicates."

Present your ideas to your target customers in a way that they are inspired to sell themselves. Your customers are going to be the best people to inspire themselves. People will buy from themselves nine out of ten times, so the key is learning how to get them to sell it to themselves. Learning the Fuess Method will provide the insight you need to inspire your customers, friends and colleagues to buy what it is you're selling.

If you can sell, you can influence people. Be careful.

It's a gift to be able to lead, inspire and influence people. If it's a gift, then you have to use the gift responsibly. If you can influence people, you must be careful about what you influence them to do. Your influence should be something that enables you to sleep well at night.

Skill in sales can be used as a dagger or in a way that is positive and helpful. The 'take care and be responsible' component was developed over time as we recognized just how much we were influencing people. The more we were influencing them, the more we realized that we needed to be very careful about how we did so.

Warning: this sales art can become too much of an intimate interaction than is appropriate for the situation. Remain professional.

This is powerful stuff, and it's going to make you stand out, whether that's professionally or personally. If used in the wrong way, it can be a negative. It's a blessing to have the skill, but it can be a curse if you misuse it. You have to realize that developing this skill comes with great responsibility because it does go below the surface. And when you get below the surface, it's powerful, and you must use that power for good.

It can take us deeper than perhaps we're accustomed to going. As a result of that, if you're not yet skilled at going deeper, you're going to experience situations that can be uncomfortable or even dangerous. A lot of men and women are simply not used to hearing each other. When you go down a path using that male-female scenario, your interaction can quickly become more intimate than intended. And intentions can easily be misperceived.

Say, for example, that you're involved in a professional discussion with a customer around bringing your product to their company. Because your customer feels heard, she could begin to divulge personal information that isn't entirely relevant to the discussion. This can start off with an occasional comment and can escalate to more information being shared that can be considered to be of a private nature. Or perhaps the information is disparaging to another member of the customer's company.

Believe me, it happens. Quite easily in fact, because when people feel heard, they want to talk. Sometimes we don't realize how much we're saying until it's too late. When practicing the Fuess Method, you must learn how to maintain a 10,000 view of the conversation. If your interaction does become too intimate and you need to back out of it to a degree, it's important to know how to do that gracefully, and in a way that doesn't detonate the whole interaction.

The art of detaching is an important skill to have if your interactions ever become personal in a professional environment. You need to know how to be careful when going below the surface professionally. It can lead to personal territory because you're listening in a way that's more than most people are accustomed to. You're asking questions that your listener isn't accustomed to being asked. It might elicit some different ideas in their mind.

You won't walk down any of those paths, however. From the outset, you've decided that you've got your lines in the sand, and no matter what you're asking, you're applying it purely to a professional situation. Don't go there in the first place. Employ very sophisticated techniques in a professional situation.

A short recap of the Fuess Method:

- Ask the big question: Why?

- Sell higher-level ideas to people when they see a need to purchase from you and invite you on their ride.
- This is an ask-and-listen approach; it's not a tell approach.
- Sell trust, not a product or a service.
- Become skilled at listening and asking questions, and watch how the perception of the person on the other side of the table improves.
- Be fully present and in the moment to clarify what the person is saying.
- Become very attuned to the people that you're selling to.
- Use a funneling technique of asking questions to lead your customer to your answer gracefully.
- Use this method at the pace with which your customer is comfortable.
- Break your customer free from natural resistances.
- Inspire movement in a direction you want them to move in so you cannot be manipulative or malicious.
- If you can sell, you can influence people. Be careful.
- Warning: this sales art can become too much of an intimate interaction than is appropriate for the situation. Remain professional.

Anyone can Fuess

At Catapult, we have hired people who were not in sales before and using the method, we have turned them into good salespeople. We don't mind hiring people from outside our industry with no industry experience as long as they're good Play-Doh, that is good learners and good listeners. We have faith that anyone can learn to utilize the

Fuess Method effectively. Despite people having varying sales backgrounds, or no prior training at all, the method is organic and intuitive and can work anywhere at any time.

There's a broader way of thinking about it that applies not only in a sales situation but on a bigger base. The Fuess Method is really about influencing people. It's about selling ideas and concepts and influencing people, and that takes place all the time everywhere and in just about every interaction. These tools and skills become even more important when selling to your customers on a digital platform. The need for ensuring you're reaching your correct target market, utilizing the proper level of influence, and asking the right kinds of digital questions takes on a whole new level of importance in the digital realm.

LEADING BY EXAMPLE

We're going to talk about a couple of case studies so you can see the Fuess Method in action. Catapult Systems' clients are spread across a variety of industries, including oil and gas, hospitality, healthcare and government, covering just about every vertical. At some point in the not too distant past, we recognized that technology was shifting, and the needs and the appetites of our customers were changing as well.

There was first a technology shift, and then there was a customer market change, which required a shift at Catapult. Remaining relevant in a shifting market was a necessity, as was being able to showcase the shift. Our answer to that shift was to convince our executives and our employees that we had to change. To do so, we used the Fuess Method.

Our chief technology officer and chief information officer, Apollo Gonzalez, transitioned from being an application or solutions architect and began to focus on technology innovation at Catapult over his tenure with the company. He started looking at technology and discerning what we should be going after as a company. He helped come up with our innovation programs which were looking at the market and at technology, and figuring out some solutions that we can bring to market that customers need. The goal was to create solutions that would help our customers transform and then figure out how we could serve them on a monthly basis rather than a one-off basis.

Breaking free from the more traditional 'design a platform for a customer and then move on' methodology, we came up with Catapult's solution-as-a-service concept. As we illustrate the effectiveness of the Fuess Method in our case studies, you'll be reading a lot about this concept and how the Catapult team first sold their executives, their employees and then their customers on these proposed services using the sales methodology we've laid out.

The new concept was a digital transformation platform where companies could work with Catapult on a continuous basis. Instead of going to five different companies to get five different things to help a customer transform digitally, they can go with us, and we can provide them with all of the digital technology services that they need. We use electronic means for digital technologies to enhance our customers' and our employees' experience, and so we have created a dynamic set of solutions to offer.

Before we delve into our case studies to illustrate how we apply the Fuess Method, we'd like to give a quick overview of just a couple of the solution-as-a-service offerings that Catapult provides for our clients so you can follow along. For the purposes of this book, the primary content will be limited to our solutions — Fuse, Launch, Spyglass, Clive and Agile Analytics — to demonstrate how we sell each service as a solution.

The first solution our team developed is the intranet as a service called Fuse.

Intranet as a service was created from the idea that employees within organizations want to be able to communicate and collaborate with each other. Building an intranet solution that all employees could benefit from was something that we did well and had already been doing for several years. We'd done thousands of them for our clients. As we thought about intranet as a service, we decided that everybody needed an intranet because most of the companies we worked with had a lot of employees that needed to be able to collaborate to be productive and find information quickly.

After doing the research, we learned that Company A through Company Z wanted the same systems, as they had the same basic needs. The question then became why Catapult needed to rebuild the intranet every time we took on a new client. Wouldn't it be better to build it once and then offer it to each client on a monthly subscription? While that didn't sound all that sexy at first, what is sexy was that the more customers used Fuse, the smarter the system grew. It learned more and was able to help make the intranet a better solution for the employees of all our customers.

Instead of getting stale — which is the way most intranets worked — we honed in on studying how our clients were using the intranet and adapting the intranet accordingly. If we saw that many customers loved using a particular feature, we could offer it to all of our other Fuse customers. One individual company could benefit from the experience of the whole, and we thought that was worth paying a monthly fee for. That is what we had to sell our board members and employees on when we first began considering that shift.

The second solution is called Launch: managed automation as a service, which here is streamlined employee onboarding.

If you think back to your first day at a new job, you might not have had a computer or email address, maybe not even a desk, and perhaps no access to the intranet, even if you did have a machine. New employees could easily hang around for a few days with little to do and access to nothing. We asked ourselves what we could do to automate that onboarding process.

As we thought through that, we realized that in addition to a company's intranet, employees usually require access to different outside systems the company uses such as Salesforce or other cloud-based SaaS solutions. If a salesperson leaves and isn't removed from Salesforce, the company could continue to pay a monthly user fee for an employee who was no longer employed there. We realized we could automate that scenario for our customers, improving their security and maybe even saving them some money.

Then we asked what were some of the other prominent use cases out there that required automation. We realized that once we automated those systems, we could offer our service to many companies and we felt comfortable thinking they'd be willing to pay for that ease. Somebody had, however, to manage and monitor, and make it better over time. A customer may add more systems that we would then need to add their employees to and we would have to build that automation. Soon 10 automations turned into 20 automations, and the list went on to become this living, breathing thing which we refer to as managed automation as a service.

The third solution is called Spyglass, which is security and data compliance as a service.

Another one of our solutions as a service is Spyglass. Every company needs security, and every company needs to be in compliance with regulations and relevant target standards. For example, if your company processes credit cards, you have to be PCI compliant, and there are no ifs or buts about it. In the United States, you have no choice. If you are in the energy industry, there are standards that you need to adhere to in order to do business because it's regulated.

Some companies have to adhere to an industry standard. Most organizations self-impose security standards and policies. Many organizations must do both. Anytime there is a level of data security and compliance that needs to occur, someone must audit that information on a regular basis to see if they are indeed in compliance.

At Catapult, our thought was that that was quite a tedious process for IT and security departments to have to do year in, year out. We decided to commoditize that process and make it possible for companies to use Catapult to help manage and monitor data security and compliance. From a process perspective, the company receives a report with a lot of requirements on what they need to do to be compliant. Many of them, not all, are technology areas that they need to focus on to be in compliance. For example, a compliance item may be that when employees leave their computer, it requires to log them off automatically in 15 minutes. Somebody has to make sure that that is happening with all the machines individually.

A company may not have the technology or the manpower to do that. They would need to acquire that technology and implement it so they can adhere to that requirement. If not, well, they're not in compliance. If they're not in compliance, then businesses won't want to do business with them. At Catapult, we realized that compliance firms audit these companies on a regular basis, and they then require these companies to put everything in place to be successfully compliant.

We asked ourselves if we could leverage a suite of technologies to ease that process for our customers. Some companies may have already purchased technology to help them do those sorts of things, but they hadn't implemented them, or they didn't know how to use them. We can implement our technology, and the technologies that we support, but we can also help customers with whatever technologies they have as well so that they're always in compliance and not susceptible to hacks or things of that nature from the outside world.

We leverage best-of-breed technologies and install, configure, and manage those technologies. We provide an interface that allows our customers to capture all of the compliance rules that they need to adhere to in order to be in compliance so they can hold themselves accountable. We provide some process, management, monitoring, implementation and configuration of their entire data-security compliance function within the company.

A newer and currently private offering is Catapult's internal chatbot, Clive.

Clive is our internal chatbot — our Alexa or Siri — that we are rolling out for our account executives currently. Clive accesses a wealth of information about anything related to an offering that we have and how it may be associated with other offerings, technology and Catapult's methodology or process. It's the collective knowledge of everything Catapult. We often refer to Clive as "he", but to avoid confusion, we will use "it" in this book.

Our account executives have to deal with all of the different solutions and services that we have to offer, which are evolving all the time. It's quite hard to keep up with what we have, why we have it, what's the purpose of it, and how we can explain it in four sentences or fewer to a potential client. We created Clive to address that need with the sales corporate-business function. If our account executives have a question about any of our solutions as a service, they have the ability to get on their phone and text a question to Clive, and it answers the question.

When they ask Clive a question, it provides them with the information that they need, which is excellent for our account executives when they need to get some information on the fly while they're talking to clients. Because it's artificial intelligence, Clive gets smarter each and every day. Clive, a year from now, will be increasingly more valuable than Clive today. We are continually updating Clive, as we work together to roll it out across the salesforce.

Agile Analytics provides companies with actionable information on an ongoing basis.

This offering is for customers who want to gain insights from data: an insight delivery service. Analytics looks at the pure numbers and analyzes the data that we've been able to gather. Analytics is useful but not nearly as good as insights. We could tell a customer that they have a problem, but we didn't help them to solve that problem. Wouldn't that be more valuable? Therein lies the difference between the two. One is informational; the other insightful. One is analytical; the other prescriptive.

Customers can access this service with a subscription, and they'll receive analytics in easy-to-consume formats. It makes it possible for them to make decisions faster because they can see results on a dashboard. When the customer is ready to ask the next set of questions, we're there to give her answers. She gets the data; she sees the results. We help her evaluate and show her real value regarding the data and the insights. We're always sharing new insights. We hold workshops. We itemize the things from the workshop that we heard and think are important. Then we define it in more detail. We develop it. We deploy it. Then we just keep iterating that. What's the next thing they want to do? It's somewhat like eating potato chips, except more useful.

When we digitally transformed Catapult, we had to develop, recruit, and embed this digital thinking across our company.

This is an important point because we first had to understand our customers' pain before we set about solving it for them. As we were going through our own digital transformation process, we wanted all of our employees to understand and experience the process. We educated them on how our new business model was going to transform our business and make life better for everyone — our customers as well as our employees. We made sure they knew we were going to leverage our employees' skills and services across many new concepts we were developing.

I'll get into more detail in a minute, but we had to sell our executive team and employees on our idea that we wanted to build an 80 percent solution to our intranet offering and customize only 20 percent for each new client. Before our shift, we would create a contract with a customer, build something for six months, receive a lump-sum payment and leave. The proposition we were giving to our employees was that instead, we were going to create a contract around something we'd already built. Then we'd build just a little bit more on it, make it better every month, and provide our customers with customization services every month for a fee. That resonated with everybody.

Rather than build individual intranets for customers over and over, we wanted to provide services and charge monthly. We knew this would be a huge benefit and a good selling point. The principle we proposed to our firm was the 80/20 rule where we could build a solution once, deploy it many times, and benefit from higher margin services that we were offering. That was obviously very appealing once the executive team and our employees understood they would get continuous benefit from it.

As we were formulating it and putting it together and thinking through the types of solutions, there was an excitement at Catapult growing around wanting to belong to that 'cool group' of kids. Everyone — from our employees to our executive team — sensed that this would be a more innovative approach and technology that would help us win new business, where we hadn't won business before with our traditional offerings. We already had managed services in place as we were going through this transition, so we were able to share with them that we knew that a subscription-based managed service on a monthly basis would produce higher margins.

We knew we had to be inclusive in offering the commitment to change demonstrated by the leadership; in acknowledging that the old ways were not working and we needed to shift to remain relevant in developing, recruiting, and embedding digital thinking across our company. We knew we first had to educate everyone on how the shift would transform the business and make life better for everyone. Then we had to foster excitement and cultivate the cool factor of being part of the oncoming innovation. And we had to demonstrate the financial incentive for the transformation.

One principle we adhered to was consistency to the model while providing an outlet for change. We wanted to build our model in such a way that it could mature, innovate, and adapt based on the changing landscape. That way we wouldn't be in the same predicament five years in the future with our customers using a stale intranet.

Catapult has designed a series of Fuess points to get both their own employees and customers on board when selling their solutions as a service:

- Be inclusive so that everyone in the company feels heard and feels invested.
- From the top levels of management all the way down, demonstrate commitment to the change.
- Acknowledge that there are better ways of doing business and that a shift is necessary to maintain relevance. Embrace the inflection point.
- Amalgamate that digital thinking across the company and weave together a process that makes a transformation better for everyone.
- Foster excitement and cultivate the 'cool' factor of being part of the innovation.
- Illustrate the financial incentive of the transformation.
- Acknowledge that digital transformation allows more emphasis on the customer, which will create a deeper working relationship with clients.
- Stay consistent but be adaptable by sticking to the envisioned business model while also building avenues for innovation.
- Everyone has a role. Transformation presents an excellent opportunity for employees to develop their skills and knowledge base further, while at the same time benefiting the organization and its customers.

- People like to be trained and relevant and have sparkly resumes, and that's one way of appealing to your employees.

Continue on to read about how we used the Fuess Method to sell our services to our executive team, our employees and finally, our customers.

SELLING THE BIG CONCEPT TO THE EXECUTIVE TEAM

FUSE: INTRANET

For the purposes of this book, there are three selling scenarios we will discuss:

- selling to your internal audience;
- selling outside of your company to your customers;
- selling to the customers of your customers.

Sometimes, before you can move forward, you have to sell to those around you. Our first solution as a service is an intranet called Fuse, which is a perfect example of how we had to sell internally to our executive team and employees. When we developed the idea of Fuse, it was important to get everybody on board to manage and guide them during our transition. Anytime you go for something new and innovative, you're going to have to bring people along your innovation curve because you all have to believe in the direction you're going. Internal selling has to happen to get your team on the same page with your future direction. How we did it wouldn't be different from any other company wanting to transform digitally, as we each use the same tools because most companies have similar needs.

To get a short and concise appreciation for the history, at first, we had nothing built. Like other companies, we first communicated internally through email, and then later by using an intranet technology called SharePoint.

It allowed us to do things that email couldn't, such as saving and sharing documents without sending them over email and creating searchability of documents. It worked so well that our customers also wanted it, so we built about 1,000 one-offs using the SharePoint platform for customers. Well, our intranet at Catapult got quite stale. It didn't adapt to the changing business landscape or to the way the younger set entering the job market was used to working.

We recognized the need to shift and transform our business to a new age of technology; to the second machine age. We wanted to go into more of an IP-led, managed-service- subscription-based model. We thought to switch to intranet as a service, which would become the first of our solutions as a service that we envisioned offering to our customers. Instead of taking six months to build out something that we had already built 500 times, we would build it one time as far as we could build it — or 80 percent — and then customize the last 20 percent for each new customer. Then we would offer continuous improvement services. Our account manager would work with that customer to look at analytics and other data to improve their employee portal productivity and engagement solution continuously.

Our intranet as a service defined the beginning of what is now our strategy, which is to sell our solutions as a continuous service. This shift shines a whole new light into digital transformation, and to what companies now hire us to do for them. At the beginning, though, we had to illustrate and build an entire business and mental picture for the executive team and our employees so that they could understand the value of this new way of doing things in a digital age, as well as the importance of undergoing digital transformation.

First, I had to Fuess our executive team.

The initial concerns from some of the executives were around our traditional business model. Before our digital transformation, we talked to the customer and explained that we could build an employee portal solution that would help improve productivity and engage their employees. The customer would then ask to learn more, and our technical sales people would walk them through the cases. Then they would ask to see it in action. Could we show it to them? Could we demo an example of how it worked? They'd love it and ask us to build it for them. We'd create a statement of work, and it would take us six months to build, and it would cost anywhere from $250,000 to $500,000. Then we'd implement it and walk away.

For an executive who's used to selling a six-month contract for $500,000 to be told we were going to sell the same thing, but now we were only going to charge $10,000 a month, you can see how there was some initial resistance. We paid our people in our business units and regions based on the old model, and then we told them that we were moving in a new direction with a new financial structure.

We had to take a step back and explain that if we build 80 percent of the intranet one time, implement it for the customer, and charge them a monthly fee, then we were always going to get that monthly fee. For the first customers that we'd win, we probably wouldn't make any money. But when we got to the third, fourth, 10th and 20th customer, we wouldn't have to build that intranet solution all over again each time because we already had it. All we were going to do was flip the switch or press the button, and they get the 80 percent, and we customize the remaining 20 percent. At that point, we would have higher profit margins.

Establishing the why

To get the executives on board for that shift was a challenge all the way around, as there was a lot of fear for different reasons within the executive team. The executive team is naturally very sharp, and they're trained to think about how any move would affect the company's bottom line. They are also trained to consider how any move might affect the employee morale across the organization. They tend to get set in their ways. Their primary question was "This is how we've always done it, so why would we do it any differently?" Naturally, that was a great question and a familiar one to any company considering the need to shift and transform.

I had to create the belief in the pain because it hadn't yet hit us. Believe me when I say that it was uncomfortable and strange to stand in front of my executive team and say that I believed a freight train was coming down the tracks, and though we couldn't see it right now, here was the evidence I had that it was headed our way. I asked that anybody who had a different view to challenge my assertion so we could have a robust dialogue around this; opening the floor for them to sell themselves on their ideas.

I had to get them to see and believe in the freight train in the dark tunnel coming our way. That wasn't a great thing for me to share with the executives running the company. But it was vital for me to do so because only once we could understand the pain together would we be able to come up with solutions around it. What I did was leave plenty of gaps and gray areas so that the team together could develop the solution. (We'll go into greater detail about a group Fuess in the chapter on advanced method.)

Leaving gray areas was a Fuess Method technique that I used as opposed to approaching our executives and saying, "I want to come to market with a new solution offering I have, and it's going to make a lot of money for us." That wouldn't have worked. Why? Because it wouldn't have been their idea. Instead, we needed to walk down the yellow brick road and explore together. I said I sensed pain on the horizon and believed there were new technologies and new ways of thinking about our business that required stepping away from how we'd always done it before.

I went on their ride.

I asked them to do this together with me and presented an example of what I thought could be our first foray into the new Catapult Systems. I presented them with the concept of Fuse, purely as an example, and asked them to look at solving this problem using the Fuse scenario. Because I didn't say we were going to build Fuse, only that we needed to have an example scenario to work on to figure out what to do, it left the field open to ideas, and the conversations happened.

I used a questioning scenario to sell them on their idea.

At that time, we didn't yet have a name for Fuse. We didn't call it a solution as a service, though we were already heading in that direction. As a company, we weren't yet thinking about recurring revenue related to our intranet. By choosing a test scenario to explore — which for us is the best way — by the time we were finished having robust discussions and explorations around Fuse as the test scenario, naturally, everybody's fingerprints were on it. They grew increasingly excited about the Fuse scenario in particular.

I used a technique called 'taking the marshmallow off the table' which is often used as part of the Fuess Method. In his book *Let's Get Real or Let's Not Play*, Mahan Khalsa references the famous Walter Mischel study performed during the 1960s at a preschool at Stanford University. Children were left alone with a single marshmallow on the table, while the researcher ducked out, telling the child that if they could refrain from eating the single marshmallow, they would be rewarded with two marshmallows when the researcher returned. Khalsa references this study to explain how consultants must "move off the solution", or resist the immediate solution that has been placed on the table, and instead ask questions of the customer that their solution is meant to solve.

I'd created a vision around how we could dodge the freight train coming down the track, and said we needed to use something as an example and I'd just randomly selected intranet, but I could have selected any solution in our business to focus on. After we finished the test scenario, I scrapped what we just did, explaining that we only needed to decide what we were going to do first. That was a way of 'taking the marshmallow off the table', which got them all wanting to put the marshmallow back on the table. In essence, through reverse psychology, they all wanted to bring Fuse back to life. They'd just spent hours putting together the test scenario, and they were in love with their ideas, so why would they do anything else?

I never took credit for the idea of designing and selling Fuse to customers.

At certain junctures, whether you're the CEO of a company or the head of a household or wherever you're the top banana, you have to, as part of your job description, lead people through the wilderness. You take any group of any size, and you'll never have 100 percent buy-in. But you win if they have enough faith in you as a leader, and more importantly — and this is key — enough belief in their own ideas.

It took more than a couple of meetings to get some people on board as they had to make a leap of faith. They became willing to step out there. We had to build a feeling of camaraderie and investment, taking the opportunity to be the sideline cheerleader and coach. Once we'd gone through the exercise and laid it all out there, they became so interested in it that they were willing to assume the risk. Why? Because they'd fallen in love with their own idea of Fuse. I couldn't take credit for leading them there, as that would have destroyed their investment in creating their solution, as well as their trust.

Fuessing our employees was our next step.

At first, our employees, to be quite honest, were frightened of Fuse. A fair chunk of them had been doing classic consulting projects for our customers for many years. It put food on their tables, provided them with a very nice income, and they were able to use the skill sets they enjoyed using. Then they heard me, their CEO, saying that we were going to do something completely different.

We had a couple of team members that were initially on the fence, but a majority bought in from the get-go. Some employees felt they needed to know more about the value, the upside and the benefits. Mentally, most of them got it, but emotionally, they were still working through the proposed change. Then we had a couple of outright detractors.

I established the why.

We had to do a lot of market research to understand what the service was going to be, rather than whether it was the right model for us or not. Fuse was the first subscription service we developed. It was an easy choice because we'd already done many intranet projects over the years and were well-versed in the consulting aspects of intranets and what it took to be successful. We only had to define the service that complemented our background and experience, and that became the Fuse solution. What we're selling and holding ourselves accountable to is the services component – the ongoing support, continuous improvement and management of that particular solution.

I told them from the outset that the mission was to commoditize the thing they did for our customers. I said not to worry as we were going to win on volume and they would still get to use the same skill sets plus they would get to develop new skill sets. But we weren't going to start from scratch anymore. We were going to build an intranet gold code, a world-class intranet, and we were going to keep it sparkly and shiny with the latest technologies and the latest features. But we were going to give it away to the customer.

Our employees worried that they might not be needed anymore. They had to take a leap of faith with us, and I had to prove to them each step along the way that they were needed. They worried that if we were commoditizing what they did, and no longer charging for what they did, why we would continue paying their salary.

An employee benefit to offering Fuse as a solution as a service was the potential for increased productivity and creativity from our employees. When our employees do these projects over and over from scratch, it becomes rather monotonous for them, as 80 percent is always precisely the same. I was able to share that now that we were going to bend the rules on how others compete against us, at the same time we would get to allow our employees to do the nifty work, not just the rinse-and-repeat tedious chores.

There were some detractors at first; not detractors as it relates to the technology, but detractors regarding the actual business model. Some didn't understand how we would make money using that model. There was one employee in particular who was skeptical. The feedback from him was that we were a consulting company, so why were we going to develop an IP, sell that IP, and support it on an ongoing basis. His thought process was that we were not that kind of company. We were a consulting company, not a product company with some services capabilities. What he failed to understand initially was that all along we wanted service as a solution to be our calling card.

I went on their ride with all of their experiences in launching Fuse.

Jeff Dalton, one of Catapult's principal consultants, says, "First, I was kind of skeptical, not about Fuse in particular, but solution as a service as a new model. How was that going to change and how was everything going to feed it? I was skeptical, but I believed in David, and I believed in his vision. Once he explained it to me in a one-on-one, I said, 'I know this is going to be hard. If nothing changes, nothing changes, but I know we've got to try something different.'" Jeff asked essential questions, such as what the great differentiator for Catapult in the market was; why customers would choose Catapult over any of the other 50 consulting companies in the market; and why we were different.

Other companies can deliver great technology but we were going to do it differently, and that was why it was going to be beneficial. Jeff remained a little skeptical that we could change, seeing how we get in our own way like most everybody else does, whether it's on a personal level or an organizational level. Overall, Jeff's resistance went quickly because he considered himself a joiner and figured he would do what he could do to make Fuse work.

Jeff shared that one of the reasons companies have associate disengagement is because it's easy for an associate end-user to think their contribution doesn't matter that much. It's not that it doesn't matter, just that it hasn't been emphasized. We haven't set up systems that allow that contribution to matter demonstrably. To a degree, Fuse does that. It continues to be part of the story that Jeff now tells about Fuse.

Nick Patterson is also a principal consultant at Catapult. When he was first introduced to Fuse as a subscription service, he was taking on a leadership role in the Denver area and had a lot of people who were extremely skeptical about Fuse. He admits that the company even lost some employees who didn't like the new direction of becoming more focused on managed services like Fuse. While we wouldn't be less focused on traditional consulting, the transition was clear that this would be the company's new direction.

"The idea of Fuse was exciting for me, but I was very skeptical. I once had a conversation with David about Fuse in which I voiced my concern that we were going to get it wrong. If we tried to do it too quickly, it wouldn't have enough though, and it needed to be done right because we wouldn't get a second chance. I was very concerned because at the time the industry was going development first, and Fuse, being a cloud-based product, was not going to be a good long-term direction."

When we decided to change our business model to be based more on subscription, first we implemented it ourselves so that we could prove it was very good and what we were telling our potential customers would be true. Because we were using the intranet as a service, moving forward was all predicated on our solutions as a service, with intranet as a service being the first one that we created.

Nick thought the concept was a good idea and was ready to buy in. "What I was concerned about was that at the time, we had a company culture that was a lot about 'fail fast'. We had a lot of great ideas and would dig into them, but if they didn't work, we'd pivot and change direction very quickly. We'd done that in several other corporate-wide initiatives," he says. "I thought if we started too fast on Fuse, we'd have issues and abandon it and I didn't want that to happen. I thought it was a good idea, and I wanted to see it succeed, so I was concerned about how we would execute."

When we started using intranet as a service at Catapult, we didn't get many complaints or arguments. We said it was a new way we were going to implement, price, and support our customers. That was the difference, and there was some friction there — not just with our executive team, but our employees as well. Our employees had concerns, as did some of our executives. But we kept trudging along.

Liam Collopy, Catapult's Chief People Officer, leads the HR department responsible for our employee engagement efforts. Liam says, "When we determined that we were moving to Fuse, I was a bit hesitant to take on that initiative. I thought Fuse would pose many of the same challenges we had historically faced with managing and updating our intranet content, but Fuse was a whole new ball game. The real magic with Fuse is that it allows the updating and managing of content and information to be decentralized. That was a game changer."

Liam said that the new analytics provided them with a view into which parts of the intranet employees would go to and utilize the most. We have analytics reports that didn't exist before. We can look at the information on our intranet and see that the expense reports and consulting templates sections are highly visited, how many employees are reading our latest press releases, and which parts of the intranet they're not using. We can drive usage or determine the value of specific content by asking for feedback from our employees based on these analytics.

The Fuse portal is the communication vehicle for the company, and everything goes through there, so it's a living, breathing thing. We have a revolving announcement scroll where you can see the different things going on in the company, press releases and up-to-date information, such as anniversaries, birthdays and upcoming company meetings. All of our information is posted there. We also have a mobile version of Fuse for our cell phones. If there's a hurricane coming and we want to provide information to our Houston employees on work procedures or shelter options, we can announce it via an update that gets pushed straight to their phones. It's quite progressive stuff, and it connects our employees to the organization on a variety of levels.

That's where I painted the vision for Catapult's employees over and over with each customer win. We showed them the benefit to the customer, the benefit to Catapult and the benefit to individual employees working on the solutions. Today, a couple of years after launching Fuse, we have no more doubt as to the business model or how it affects the type of work we do.

Everyone is onboard now.

Liam adds, "Fuse is selling well, but when you sell a service like this, the real proof is in the renewals. As we have very high renewal rates, that proves that Fuse has real value for our customers. When we deliver a Fuse solution to a customer, the team knows the results are predictable, and we're going to have a very happy customer. We know that what we're doing for our customer will change how they communicate and interact with their employees."

Now we get to walk into a customer's office and say we're going to customize their intranet. With 80 percent of it prebuilt, our employees get the pleasure of designing the 20 percent that's interesting and customized. That means we have many more exciting projects for our employees to work on, and that was the whole concept of the commoditization and winning on volume. Today that has absolutely played out, so much so that as we introduce our new solutions — and we have seven or eight additional ones now — we don't have to go back to the drawing board with each of our employees and resell them on why it's good for them. They've seen it work, so now they focus on the solution and how to make it great for our customers. We're genuinely past that initial stage.

Liam notes that Catapult's employee satisfaction and productivity increased after the firm implemented Fuse internally. "Part of the program for me was not only getting an effective intranet but measuring employee engagement. I have another solution as a service tool I use as well that allows our employees to provide anonymous feedback directly to me on things that are going on in the company or with them individually. If something is critical or of high priority, I'm able to answer directly in real time. We have a level of communication and engagement in our organization that we never had before implementing Fuse, and our staff turnover is as low as it's ever been."

Apollo's participation

During the initial transition, Apollo gathered the salespeople, internal support and technical support folks together. "I put up a website with the image of Six Flags Fiesta Texas, and after I went through the website, I asked the team what they'd seen. They answered that they'd seen people on rides screaming their heads off — all the usual fun; amusement park stuff. Then I took them to the Disney website and asked what they saw. They described smiling parents with kids, kids hugging Mickey Mouse, a princess holding a little girl's hand, and a girl with a big smile on her face."

On one site it looks like everybody's terrified. On another site, it seems like everybody's having the time of their lives. On one site, you see rides, because Six Flags is selling the product — which is the ride itself. They're selling that part of the experience. Disney is selling the actual experience. They're selling the emotional aspect, which is the service that they provide. If you go to Disney, you don't have to worry about anything.

Apollo explained to the team that Catapult's solution as a service is Disney. All the other software companies out there that say they do what we do concerning an intranet solution, a security solution or an automation solution — they're Six Flags. Therein lies the difference between our value proposition and theirs. You could go to Six Flags and see people lining up for their rides. But Disney's on a whole different level. They can charge twice as much for their Diet Cokes and tickets into the park, and you're going to pay it. Why? Because of that experience and the service you get when you go to Disney.

"That's what we were trying to bring with our solutions as a service," Apollo explains. "We had a dissenter who initially didn't understand that distinction, which was probably our fault and we should have done a better job of articulating that aspect. That's really important for any digital transformation. Whoever is the group leader has to make sure they nail that part of it, or you'll end up with a lot of dissenters. As far as the digital transformation goes, they won't understand what it is and where they fit."

The dissenter's struggle was that he spent his life doing the Six Flags 'fun ride' thing, but now he was being told we were going to do the Disney 'experience' thing. He was a consultant who'd successfully built solutions over and over again from the ground up for each customer, and then was finished. Now we presented a new world where we'd already built 80 percent of the product. We might tweak and customize another 20 percent, but we were moving into a role where we would manage and support our product on an ongoing basis. Our dissenter didn't know how he'd fit in that world.

Today, when we hire anyone, we go through a pretty robust onboarding process where they learn about what Catapult is and who they can be at Catapult. We explain our vision, and we explain solution as a service, and what it means to employees, and how they can excel. We learned from our earlier mistakes about not being crisp on the value proposition.

"We did get our dissenter on board when we started to see the success with our new direction. Success and winning breeds that process of either you need to dial in and be a part of it, or you need to do something else," Apollo says. "Our dissenter was eventually seduced by the fact that over time our solution as a service worked, and also by the fact that the area that he was responsible for benefited from the success. His area started to see more revenue as they increased what they were doing regarding sales. His pockets started to get fatter, and money is always a big influencer. David does a masterful job with always ensuring that all the executives are pulling in the same direction by uncovering the challenges, bringing them to the light of day, and then allowing the team to work together to solve them."

I never took credit.

Nick Patterson said that once it was implemented inside the company, Fuse cracked the door open across many other technologies besides intranet-focused technologies, explaining that implementing Fuse needed to be very standard. "Anybody needed to be able to come on board and be able to implement Fuse and have the things they needed and know the conversation," he said.

From a deploying intranet standpoint, it forced us to standardize all of those processes, and come up with a common code base, which then showed the value of doing that across the entire organization. That has been leaked into other technologies that may not be directly related to Fuse or any of the other service offerings. Fuse set the stage for that and has, even at an upper management level, everybody thinking of how we can be more efficient at delivery and sharing information with our clients. It's definitely changed the personality and the culture within Catapult to do more of that and share more information across the organization.

GETTING YOUR EMPLOYEES ROWING IN THE SAME DIRECTION

When we created Fuse, Launch, Spyglass, Clive and our other offerings, we didn't create them in a vacuum. We established a working group comprised of people from all across the company. We included salespeople, marketing folks, consultants and one or two executive stakeholders that formed a working group or a solution committee. For every solution that we have brought to market, there's a group focused on looking at what it is and understanding its impact. Our marketing team and HR does an outstanding job of taking what it is and essentially selling it internally so that everybody knows what it is, understands its value, and knows how it can help our customers. We use it, but ultimately, we also want our customers to use it because that's how we create income.

We have a whole innovation process that eventually feeds into another group that's responsible for the execution of it. There's an intersection between those two. We share market testing and working with our internal consultants. Our people out in the field know the customers, work with customers, and know what the customers want. We bring them into the process so that they can understand. We believe in inclusiveness rather than the ivory-tower approach. This method of educating our team to inform others helps tremendously when rolling out new products.

Our internal chatbot, Clive, that we are developing is designed to assist our sales executives when they're working with customers. There are two important reasons for using Clive as an example of the Fuess Method in process. One, we first had to sell Clive to our internal team before we were able to move forward in development. And two, Clive is designed to emulate the Fuess Method of asking questions by allowing our sales executives to use it right in front of a potential customer.

Selling Clive internally

Clive is still relatively new. We presented the concept of Clive to the executive team by first identifying our problem. We had a lot of solutions and a lot of sales people and a lot of collateral but no good way of bringing them all together. Most salespeople like to use their phones when they're in a situation where they're pitching. They're not about to go fumbling through a stack of paper while trying to find valuable information for the potential customer in front of them. They needed access to information from their phone in a way that would help them sell.

We presented the challenge and the problem to the executive team and then revealed Clive as an artificial intelligence chatbot that through text would allow our sales executives to ask questions, such as what is Fuse, what is Launch and what is Spyglass, in front of potential customers.

The executive team was wowed before the presentation was complete. Identifying the problem and presenting Clive as an idea for a solution left a lot of gray space for the executive team to jump on. Immediately, the conversation leaped to what else we could do with it. To the team, a concept like Clive made complete sense as it was precisely what even our customers were asking for.

After the executive team bought in, we were able to get on the phone with some of our sales executives and walk them through Clive, what it is, what it does, what it responds to. We worked with our marketing department because they were responsible for providing Clive with the content it needed to get smarter. Those three things happened in that order. When our sales people have questions now, they can ask Clive. If Clive doesn't know an answer to their question, we are notified, and our marketing department can give it those answers so that it can be smarter based on the questions it's unable to answer. This constant feedback loop is continually helping Clive to develop its own capability.

We have a quality assurance team that works on Clive to make sure that the information it's feeding back is correct. The machine is continually getting smarter, and that's the idea behind it. Somebody is always taking a look at its data sets and making sure that they're accurate because Clive can pick up data from various places and some of those sources could provide inaccurate information.

When Clive is asked a question, and it doesn't know the answer, someone will get notified, and then it's a little more proactive. It doesn't sound proactive because somebody's doing something to trigger this event, but over time as you start asking questions, Clive gets smarter. It can say, "I should be able to answer that question. Let me see if I can find some answers." Then Clive can let the marketing department know that somebody asked a question. Then the marketing department can go ahead and push those recommendations out. I know that gets somewhat scary; it sounds like artificial intelligence going awry. But that's a future capability that we could build into it.

Clive as a Fuesser

Regarding application to the Fuess Method, Clive provides relevant information for our account executives. To be more specific, to succeed in executing on the method we've been talking about, Clive requires refined questioning — a key component of the Fuess Method.

Think of Clive as a funnel. At the top of the funnel would be the beginning of the usage of the method — or the beginning of a dialogue. Those questions might start out as fairly generic, open-ended and high-level. With each question or each interaction, the questions become more specific as you move down the funnel. Clive helps support the Fuess Method, as it gives the right information at the right time. This may help our sales executives in future to slow down to ensure that they're not trying to rush customers through the Fuess Method.

There's some magic here that is worth pointing out. It's very tempting to go straight from the top to the bottom of the funnel in one fell swoop. You may be right in knowing after a couple of high-level questions precisely what the answer is going to be and head right to it. The problem with that approach is you don't take the participant along with you. They don't yet see Point A to Point Z, because they're new to the information.

You may see it because you've done this many times, but if you're going to succeed in getting them to paint their own picture, to come up with their own idea, and ultimately, to sell themselves on their own idea, it's imperative that you move slowly through this funnel. Take one step at a time. Don't go straight from Step 1 to Step 10 if 10 is the end of the conversation and where you might make a sale of an idea or concept.

People need to be able to bring themselves along at a self-paced speed that works for them, something we will discuss in the Advanced Method chapter. We make decisions at different paces. Some people like to make decisions slowly and thoughtfully while being very analytical. Others prefer to buy on emotion at first glance. They know at first glance if they want what you're selling or not, and they either buy or move on. It's important to move along at the pace of the person you're selling to. You'll find that the people who are the New-York-in-a-hurry kind of people will hurry through the process. That's fine, as it's their pace you're establishing.

The Clive bot is designed to provide the right information at the right time so that the user of the method can ask more and more refined questions. It operates on a real-time basis, which is like having someone speaking in your ear via a teleprompter. You don't have to memorize everything; it's being served right to you at the right time.

You do have to know the right questions to ask Clive to relay the right questions or information to the person you're selling to. It's serving up data, so the person who's running the method with the customers has to be able to ask the right questions of Clive, as well as ask the right questions of the customer. The person learning the method has to put everything in context, which means it requires a fair degree of art and a reasonable degree of practice.

The chatbot can help your sales team slow down in case they might get overeager and try to rush the process. You can tune it to make sure you're not skipping too far ahead to the answer. It's very tempting, when you know what the answer is, to say, "Here's the answer and assume I'm correct because I've done this a thousand times." It's not a very effective way to sell, and it's not following the Fuess Method. Remember, you get buy-in when you don't sell what's not needed, you're careful in how you wield your influence, you ask the right questions, and you allow your prospect to fall in love with their own idea.

It's better to treat every situation from scratch and walk them through at their own pace. Clive can be tuned to ask clarifying questions, and not to jump from Point A to Point Z. If you ask the wrong question too early, Clive will say, "Hey, I think there's some more information that needs to be uncovered before we go on to that question."

There's an old example that when asked for a drill, you shouldn't assume that the asker necessarily wants to drill a hole. You should ask what they want to use the drill for. You may discover that they have some sort of unique thought in mind. If you find out they want to drill a hole, you might find out more about that hole before you say that a drill is the best thing to use for that hole. There may be a better tool to use for it.

It's a natural tendency to think you don't want to ask questions because people are going to get annoyed. What you find is if you skillfully ask questions, people appreciate it. They appreciate that you're really trying to help them find the right solution rather than just say, "Here's a drill," because they asked for a drill. That's the essence of how Clive has been tuned.

Examples of clarifying questions

Let's take the kind of question our sales executives might be asked when selling our solutions as a service, such as what different languages can be used to build a particular application. There are a lot of different computer languages out there, such as Digital Basic, .Net, HTML, Java or Python, and they each exist for different uses. If you ask Clive that question, it would likely answer, "Before I answer that question, can you help me understand what type of application your customer is looking to build?"

In other words, why do you need a drill? Your response may be, "It's an internal-facing application, meaning it's going to exist on an intranet, and it's going to be served up using a web page, and there's going to be a lot of content like videos and chat, and those kinds of features in it."

Clive might say, "Okay, that's very helpful. Based on your description of this particular application, there are a few different languages that may make sense. Of those, HTML is one, Digital Basic is another, and .Net is another. To decide which of those three toolsets would be most appropriate to recommend, I'd like to find out some more information. What kind of technology does your customer typically use internally?"

Your answer might be, "Well, they're typically in a Microsoft shop."

Clive could say, "If they're in a Microsoft shop, then Visual Basic or .Net would tend to be perfect tools to use. Can you tell me if their developers understand object-oriented programming?"

You might say, "No, they're really not into object-oriented things. They try to keep it simple."

Clive would say, "Based on everything that you've described, my recommendation is they use Visual Basic to write that application."

Keep in mind, this is happening in the potential customer's presence, so you're bringing them along the funnel without them knowing. The above interaction would be the sort of clarifying questions that Clive could do, which is very artistic and similar to what you would want a sales executive to do as they're selling ideas using the Fuess Method.

If you ask Clive, "What is Fuse?", Clive will respond, "This is what Fuse is." If you want more details about Fuse, it'll give you a link. That link will send you to a website or to a page or a PDF where you can get a lot of detail. You can share that link with a potential customer.

In other words, Clive is designed to lead the sales executive through the funnel, who in turn Fuesses the potential customer as the entire interaction takes place front and center.

DOING THE RIGHT THING AT THE RIGHT TIME

CHARACTERISTICS OF A SALES EXECUTIVE

Speed in assessment a crucial characteristic

What we sell at Catapult is very complicated. There aren't so many tangible features and benefits, so our salespeople need to think on their feet and quickly. It's a requirement in our business, so the ability to follow the complexities and process them quickly so that they can apply them to the sales call as it's happening has grown increasingly important. Generally, the more complex the sale or the service of the product you sell, the more critical raw intelligence becomes.

It's very easy to get zigzagged in a sales process, so having the ability to figure out the fastest path from Point A to Point B on the fly comes into play. You can't take too much time as it can result in the buyer becoming very frustrated. A salesperson must continually be able to reassess in real time the fastest way from Point A to Point B while simultaneously allowing the client the appropriate amount of time to digest what they hear.

Some clients pick up things like boom, boom, boom, boom and they want to move at a rapid pace. Others like to think about things and that ties into being able to read your audience well. If you don't understand those cues correctly, you can become very frustrating to the person on the other side of the table. Giving appropriate absorption time based on the particular buyer, but still moving from Point A to Point B in the most expedient manner is a top skill.

You also need to understand the investment from the company side of things. Relative to how much time you're spending on a sale, you have to be able to ascertain the return of the investment that you're getting out of the time spent on that sale. Being able to size up the right amount of time that should be spent on this pursuit relative to the return on it is essential. The bigger the pursuit, the more time is spent on it.

The comfort and skill in asking questions

Some people don't want to ask questions because they feel that they're being intrusive, or their audience is going to take it the wrong way. Then some people ask questions all the time. We tell our children there's never a bad question, but there are bad ways of asking questions.

At Catapult, we look for people who are naturally gifted and curious. One of the characteristics you see in inquisitive people is that they tend to ask many questions, but they ask them in friendly ways, and that's a critical aspect of being an effective salesperson.

Salespeople need to be able to read people and to listen to other people — both what they're saying and what they're not saying. Sometimes people won't tell you what they're actually thinking. They'll hide their thoughts because they might fear you will exploit them in some way. If you can get them to feel at ease, and they think it's okay to tell you what's on their mind, then that relationship is going to be smoother.

You could ask four or five questions, and within a few minutes, your listener could be thoroughly turned off. You could shut them down, and they would walk away, hoping they never have to see you again. Or you can ask another set of questions, and they'll want to have dinner with you. There's an art in how you ask people the right question in an inoffensive way. It's a learned skill, but it's also something that can come prepackaged to a degree. We've found that you have a better Play-Doh when you find people who already know how to ask questions naturally.

Charisma is an essential trait of a salesperson, albeit a nebulous one.

There are different kinds of charisma. We could give you many examples of successful salespeople who you might be shocked are amazing at sales; if you met them at a dinner party, they might seem quiet or withdrawn. Many times, salespeople tend to have a certain look to them, and they tend to be more attractive people, yet you can probably name many examples of people who don't fit that mold.

They may not be spit-and-polished. They're not hugely charismatic. They don't tell all the funniest jokes and stories. They just seem to reach people well. They come across as the salt of the earth with a unique, humanistic quality about them that makes other people want to engage with them. This quality comes in many different varieties; it's not one cookie-cutter mold. We look for people who have some exceptional quality or qualities about them, but it varies from person to person. We look for something unique about them that is attractive, but not necessarily physically attractive.

Charisma is necessary for being able to execute sales tactics in a way that feels natural and not contrived. Some attributes lend themselves to that such as being patient, understanding, unflappable, remaining even-tempered, and allowing people to complete their thoughts and finish what they're thinking and saying. The flip side to that is you don't want to come across as arrogant. You don't want to seem like a know-it-all. You don't want to be intimidating in your knowledge of the subject. Some people are smart, and they want you to know that they're smart. That doesn't go over well when you're trying to sell. You have to remove ego from the equation.

Credibility + reliability + intimacy / self-orientation

We like the trust formula (above) in the book *The Trusted Advisor*. This is useful to drive home the point at how self-orientation works against you. There are benefits of finding ways to take actions that are selfless and make them beneficial to the Fuess Method.

One of the most fundamental concepts of the method is lack of ego, or at least the taming of it. To be genuine, the user of the method *must want* to understand the other party fully and ensure he becomes sold on his own ideas and solutions. This has the effect of the audience trusting the salesperson. The way of achieving this result is the use of a technique called funneling. Funneling is the skillful asking of questions which uncovers (as opposed to leads) predispositions towards perceived needs or solutions. This environment allows for creative thinking and brainstorming and eventually deducing the best answer.

Of course, if done correctly, the solutions will be something in congruence with the desired outcome of the user of the Fuess Method. This can be done without being sneaky, coercive or manipulative. It merely is an effective technique resulting in action or decisions being made.

They need to be very inquisitive by nature, and good at asking questions without offending the other person. They need to have that kind of insight to listen and also apply what they're hearing to ask some insightful questions in a non-offensive manner.

Recognizing when it's not time to sell

Given the set of characteristics we feel are essential to a sales executive, you should be able to determine the various reasons why you sometimes shouldn't move your buyer forward to a sale. Not everyone is your target market, despite the work you may have done to narrow your focus to customers who need what you sell. High intelligence comes in at this point because when you're employing the Fuess Method, and you realize that the person you're talking to doesn't need what you're selling, you need to disengage and then send them to other providers if you can.

There's a certain power that comes along with using this method effectively. As a user of the technique, it's important you recognize the power associated with it because you can allow people to make poor decisions to your benefit just because it was their idea, as the method enables people to be sold based on their own ideas. If you're in it for a quick sale or the money, even though they're making a poor decision, it's still their decision, and they get to own it. You can allow them to do that using the method. But do you want to?

It's a potent situation when you're using the method; the customer has the intended idea, and they start buying their idea. You need to know when to pause and say, "It's a good idea, and I've seen other people take that same approach. I actually would caution you against that decision for this couple of reasons. Here's another approach that you might consider. By the way, this isn't even a service that we provide. Here's another way of looking at it."

A comfortable and trustworthy salesperson would handle the above scenario with grace and intelligence. It's a way of building long-term trust and sacrificing short-term gain with the customer. The Fuess Method will allow people to fall in love with their own ideas. It's important to recognize that not all ideas are great. This foresight is precisely right for building trust and helping your client feel like you've got their best interests at heart.

People usually recognize when they're biting on a hook. If you're about to buy a car and you've found that car you want, you bite on it, but you can't control yourself. You might think, "I've got to have that car" or "I've got to have that house" or "I've got to have this service". And as much as you know you're being a sucker, you're falling for it, and you're still going to fall for it, so to speak. You're all bought in.

If you can put yourself in a position where you're about to make that decision to buy something in your personal life, and a salesperson on the other side of the desk can actually pause and say, "One thing you haven't considered is this, and as a result of that I might suggest you consider a different car, house or solution. I can't provide it for you. As much as I would like to sell it to you, I can't." That's when you get a customer for life. Not only is it the right and ethical thing to do, but they will come back to you every single time if they know you have their best interest at heart.

If you don't need what I'm selling, then I'm not going to sell it to you.

You should look for every opportunity to build trust with the people that you're selling to. For example, Inuit don't need ice cubes, and when you say that a person can sell ice cubes to the Inuit, that's not a good thing. You want to sell heaters to the Inuit. If what you're selling to a person isn't right for them, you either back off or connect them to another person who might be able to provide them with what they actually need. There's no better way to build long-term trust. That's how you create the clientele who come back and buy from you over time when they do have a need for what you're selling.

When you think of selling, you tend to think of the used-car salesman or the person who shows up with knives at your door. This sort of slick-talking persona can make you feel like you can't get away from them fast enough. There are plenty of those guys and gals out there, but if you can hone your craft and do it in a uniquely professional way, you can stand out from the crowd quite easily when you do it with character and integrity.

Sometimes you discover that they don't need your idea, and you have to be okay with that. Sure, you could sell ice cubes to the Inuit, but they don't need ice cubes. If you're using this method authentically, and you discover through conversation that you could probably sell someone on something that's not right for them, you should stop and say, "I don't think what I have to offer is the best for you right now, but down the line, it may be." That way you build a lot of respect and a lot of credibility and a lot of trust.

You always have to be willing to concede when what you have to offer isn't the best thing for the customer. If you know someone else who can provide the best thing, you should go that one extra step and put them together. Because you build trust and respect, they'll be a future customer. We're not the only company on the planet that provides what we provide, and sometimes customers have a relationship with someone else that is longer and deeper, so you sometimes lose out to long-standing relationships. That doesn't happen that frequently, however, as this method has a way of putting you at the front of the pack because the customer isn't used to being listened to.

Say you look at a couple, and they look like they're not equally yoked. Let's say one isn't as attractive as the other and you wonder how they ended up together. We see it all the time. You expect people to be with people who are about the same as far as physical appearances go. If you dig into it, you find out the why, which is most of the time because one will say, "I feel heard. It feels like what I'm saying is of genuine interest to her."

The Fuess Method boiled down is essentially that basic human instinct that, even if you have a business relationship with someone else, and you bought services and products from them before, maybe you don't feel entirely heard. When we come in later and use this method on you, you're going to wonder if the current relationship you have is as good as you thought it was, because we totally get you.

The most important reason for a sale: emotion

People would like to think that, in the business realm, a decision is made because it's a better product or it's a better service or it's at a better price. That's generally on the list of things that get checked along the way, but it's virtually never the entire list. There are almost always other things that are more important than price or product, or features and benefits. It's the moment you get outside of the hardcore technicals of it that you get into the emotional side of things.

People buy on emotion. Sure, in the world of sales, it's not true that 100 percent of the time people buy on emotion, but most sales are made when an emotional connection is established. For you to get the audience to connect with something emotionally, there must be a creative component that perhaps fires up their senses. They usually have to feel a strong connection to what you're selling. Those sensations are what connects them to the item or service that is being sold.

People do their investigation on the Internet, and they make comparisons, and generally, they relate to two or three of their choices. Then they decide from that short list which one to buy. Then it's the artful seller or sales organization that likely wins from that short list. Whether buying a car, procuring a business service or buying a brand new network for your company, you generally narrow your choices down to three and then decide who to buy from. Their features, text and prices are all basically the same, plus or minus some small percentage. This is where the real selling begins.

Say ten CFOs are looking to buy a piece of accounting software for a company; a scenario that sounds very black and white. Ten different CFOs narrow their list down to the same three products — Dynamics, Oracle and SAP, for example. All ten of those CFOs have done their homework. As they move to the next phase of the sales process, they realize they could buy any of those three products, and any one of them will get the job done.

Now they're faced with the decision of who they're actually going to buy from. Well, if you did the forensics after all 10 of those CFOs purchased their product, you'd discover that the deciding factor would be something other than price, features and benefits because it had already been narrowed down to three similar choices. The actual buying criteria involves something that was personal to them. It could be that they think the service would be better with one company. It could be that their brother's company used that piece of software and he was pleased with it. It could be that the salesperson was very responsive, and when they ran into an issue, they thought they would have a good advocate.

The list could be 10 different reasons, none of which were precisely the same as to why they selected what they did. Our method is intended to help in that situation by using a technique that inspires them to sell to themselves. If you can get ten CFOs to sell to themselves, they're all going to buy from themselves, because they sold it to themselves. Using our method, you're going to appeal to them in an entirely different way. Why? Because you're going to get your target customer to sell to himself.

MASTERING THOSE CHALLENGING SALES

No one ever said sales is easy. If you're selling, then you will run into some challenging sales. Even when you adhere to your ethics (or perhaps because of them), you may meet challenges. Sometimes your ethics can cause the challenges, while sometimes your ethics will be the solution.

Let's expand on where ethics and sales can collide, as they relate to the Fuess Method. Even though one of the fundamental premises of the method is that we are leading people to act and be sold on their own ideas, it's important to note that just because it's their idea does not necessarily mean that it's a good idea, or that it's what's best for them. I would advocate that ethically we must ensure that the other party is making the right decision for themselves. If we don't agree, we bring the topic up for discussion even if it doesn't benefit the method user.

Yes, we're selling, but relationships last a lifetime, and we're not swinging for the fences with a one-time sale. Our goal is to develop a deep, trusted relationship which will be mutually beneficial for the rest of time. This can only be achieved by acting ethically at all times.

Inability to try out your service or concept before purchase

If you want an email account, you can go to Google, try it out, and if you don't like it, you don't use it. It helps that it's free and you get to use it and experience it at your leisure. This is as opposed to our offerings Launch, Spyglass or Fuse. You can't try them out for free. You can't just click the button and all of a sudden you have security or sophisticated automation or an intranet. It's more complicated than that. Naturally, this means we must take care in adhering to our ethics and only selling to customers who should be consuming our services.

With Google and other services out there, you can just consume on Day 1, and then you can decide if you like it or not. A silly analogy is that we can date for a couple of days, and then we can get married. It's very quick because you could try Google out in advance. With solutions as a service, we don't have a dating period. We're basically telling our customers to marry us right away and trust us that everything is going to work out as we say. This is a big commitment! Sometimes, they say, "Wait a minute, but we didn't even date! At least with Google, we could date for a little bit before I decided whether or not I wanted to get married."

We've been working feverishly to come up with new ways to solve that problem. That's a challenge when you first embark on building solutions and services that are driven by the service. Dating a service versus a product is hard. A product's easy, but a service is more complex and challenging. Our customers must trust that we wouldn't sell them something they don't need.

The way we've come to solve that problem initially — and we're continuing to work out new ways — is to think about how we can provide customers with a way to date without spending too much money. We've started to incorporate workshops and assessments, and proof-of-concept opportunities for some of our solutions.

With Spyglass, we can go in and do a security assessment. That allows us to build a relationship very quickly with the customer, and that's basically the dating process. They see that we come in, and for quite a low cost, we do a considerable value service for them. They like what we have to tell them, and they like the deliverables, and it only takes a week or two. They're soon ready to get engaged.

We do the same thing for Launch. We know they've got a lot of processes that need to be automated, so we do an assessment to determine what is going on. That's what we have been incubating and doing to drive more interest and to build relationships faster because we lack the productization that exists with other software as a service out there. Again that's not what we are, and that's not what we're trying to sell. We're trying to sell a long-term relationship in which you want to pay us for some high-value-added concepts, and we cure all your ills with our services.

Finding the decision-maker

When meeting with potential intranet consumers, we don't necessarily lead with the option of Fuse. We start asking whether they've ever thought about leveraging SharePoint as an intranet platform and electronic-management type of platform and giving people access to upload their own data to make their jobs easier, and easier for them to get fresh and new content. Typically, that's the start of the conversation.

We might pull up a Fuse demo without actually mentioning Fuse. In most scenarios, they ask, "What is that?" and we tell them we use it as an example because it has good sample content, but this is a service we provide called Fuse. If they say they don't want to pay for another online service, then we know we're not talking to the right person. They're probably not the decision-maker, as most decision-makers know that solutions as a service save them money in the long run and are a worthwhile investment.

When selling in this way, Nick Patterson says that more often than not, potential customers will ask how the service works. "Then I can get into the details and backdoor my way into that sales conversation without them realizing it. I'm not a sales guy, so talking to them, and 'accidentally' showing it to them seems to get a better reaction from people."

Your technique may lose effectiveness.

The first time somebody uses reverse psychology on you, for example, you're likely to go for it since you've never experienced it before. If reverse psychology is what you use with your children all the time, it loses its effectiveness on them over time. There's probably a limited number of times you can successfully leverage this in a way that makes sense. Eventually, they'll catch on, and that particular method will no longer be effective.

Selling with integrity and asking all the right questions is what good selling is all about. But planting that seed and leading the person to the conclusion over and over again will after a while lose its shine. After repeated use, your audience will probably realize what's going on. This is why it's important to be well-versed in the art of sales. Being nimble on your feet, and knowing when to switch sales tactics comes in handy.

Your customer doesn't have the ability to come up with your idea.

The Fuess Method is effective for many reasons. In the right set of circumstances, it's a very non-invasive, practical approach to leading a customer to a set of conclusions without being forceful in any way. You're doing basic discovery by asking the right questions, or in this case leading questions, and having the patience to wait.

It takes great patience to wait for the customer to connect the dots on her own and figure out what would make sense and ask what if she did this or she did that. It can be challenging to sit still and wait and not jump the gun and say to her, "Given everything you've told me, this solution seems like it would make a lot of sense". It's obviously more powerful if the customer comes to that conclusion on her own.

Sometimes customers just don't connect the dots you'd like them to connect, in which case, you'll have to put your solution forward anyway. If you're selling a complex solution, the customer's not going to think of the answer on her own, no matter what, because she may have never seen it, heard of it, or thought of it before. In this case, the Fuess Method sales process isn't going to work. Some education is going to have to take place on your part. For this to be effective, the customer has to be able to envisage the solution on her own, given her own mix of historical context and data and experiences.

If it's a complex solution that the customer is unlikely to have ever heard of before, then it's difficult for this to work, if not outright impossible. If, on the other hand, the options that are in front of the customer are from a relatively known set of different options that she could choose from, she can make a choice. But then other results don't end with a sale for anybody. Sometimes, one of the customer's options is to do nothing. Or the customer can solve her problem internally or hire someone else to do it.

UNDERSTANDING YOUR CUSTOMER'S PAIN

In our first scenario, we discussed the method behind selling to an internal audience. In this second scenario, we'll cover the next step which is selling outside of your company to your customers.

The beauty behind Catapult's Launch can be explained as if this, then that. For example, you could take a picture on Instagram, email it, and then store it on your computer or phone, and then you could text it. There's nothing to keep you from doing it that way. Or you can connect Instagram to other channels and run basic scripts behind the scenes to make it happen automatically.

If you understand this simple scenario, then you can appreciate Launch, because Launch is the exact same thing but from an enterprise perspective, and the problems that it automatically solves are more enterprise business process in scope. Launch is a platform that offers several different things, including script automation, monitoring, management and security. The whole thing is running in the cloud on Microsoft Azure.

One area of those business outcomes is employee provisioning and employee deprovisioning. This means when a new employee starts on a job many things have to happen for them to be productive on Day 1. He needs passwords, access and a computer at a minimum. He may need access to and a subscription created for an outside program, such as Salesforce.

Somebody in IT will have to do all of this very tedious work manually. Now, assuming that all happens, and on

Day 1, the employee has everything he needs, what happens if six months later he quits? Somebody must then remove the employee from all those systems. A couple of weeks could go by where the employee is still getting emails, and the company is paying for memberships to websites. The account needs to be deprovisioned from all the systems that he had access to, and all of that is also done manually.

This acknowledgment taps into the customer's why. We understand their pains in having to use valuable resources and technology to handle each and every transfer of information manually.

The client has a need, and we both must believe in the pain.

The demo is the client's first impression. It looks nice, catches their eye, and causes them to think about the potential of what we offer. The initial demos done during the sales process are high level and talk about the value of automation. Once we start diving into details, the client begins to understand what Launch is, how it works, how it can fit into their organization and how it would work with what they're currently doing.

To approach that process of introducing service as a subscription as a technological resource, the conversations usually happen with IT. This makes it quite tricky because IT is generally a proud group and wants to support everything themselves and they believe that they're capable. What we've learned is that they're certainly capable of supporting employee onboarding and other processes automated by Launch. But due to bandwidth issues, they may not have the time to improve their internal processes and give them the attention it needs to stay relevant and be a resource for the organization.

We know they're smart and have the skill sets to do what it takes, but do they have the time? And that's where our solution as a service can come in, which is to tell the customer we're going to supplement their time. We have people that have these conversations and do this exact automation all the time and can help them take repetitive tasks off their plate.

Going on their ride

Another issue we often heard about from our customers was around server maintenance, such as provisioning and patching, and other things that had to be done manually, so we automated all of that too. We designed an IT package that's focused on automating the deployment, patching and management of Windows operating systems. If you have hundreds or thousands of employees, many different manual things have to happen to keep that operating system up and running efficiently all the time. If a machine isn't in compliance, we'll immediately know it and get it into compliance. We're able to help the infrastructure IT to manage, configure, patch, build and deploy Windows operating systems on employees' machines.

We let our customer know that they can evaluate these processes at any point in time. If we sell Launch to your company, then your IT department can look at the Launch interface and see all the automations that are occurring. They can see whether they were successful and which ones had problems. You can solve those problems because you know that they're happening. We're letting you know that they're happening, sometimes as soon as they happen and even before an end user — an employee in this example — knows anything happened.

Asking questions

Launch saves customers tons of time, and who doesn't want more time to focus on their company business? We're helping to manage that automation on an ongoing basis because automation occurs all the time. Every time a new person is hired, there's automation. How many new employees do you bring in each month? How many do you have to disengage from? For every employee that is either coming in or going out, something is being automated. We want to be able to see what that is and be able to adjust different factors based on what's happening and then share it with you.

Do you have the flexibility to create new automations, and to leverage existing ones? We do — and all of that is part of the value proposition and the service we offer. The reason why customers love that is that they see we've successfully run Launch with multiple customers. You can have a level of confidence that it's going to work for you because we've already done it. People like to buy things that are battle-tested, and the innovation curve doesn't factor in for things like this. Those are mission-critical processes that, if not correctly installed, can cost you a lot of money — and we're trying to save you money.

As Launch has evolved, our lead concept has become lifecycle management with the focus as the service and not automation. Certainly, automation is still part of it and a key value, but we are really trying to drive the "we will handle this for you" message rather than the "we have some automation" message.

Say you work at Hometown Hospital and you hire 1,000 new employees a month. There may be an equal number of deprovisioning happening as well. That could be several thousand automations happening each month for your company that we can take off your plate just around hiring and deprovisioning.

Then you come back to us and say, "This is working out well. We have five or six other things we would love for you to check out. Can you automate these too?"

We check them out and say, "Well, we sure can."

Then you come to us and say, "This other package you have around servers and computers and being able to set them up and configure them — we think we could use it. We're setting up new systems frequently. We do probably about 500 a month."

We say, "Fantastic. We'll get that set up for you. We're going to add another 500, and now your total automations are 2,500."

We've believed in your pain, understood your pain, and asked you the right questions to help you develop the idea that we can sell you what you need to solve your pain.

Our ultimate goal is to sell our customer the entire Digital Workplace suite because we believe in it.

Launch is just one of those solutions that when we get in, we can start talking to them about some of the other services that we offer because we understand the pain of going through digital transformation. To live in the new world, we support the idea of enterprises doing things in a new way. We are excited by the idea of how much more time our customers will have to do all these other tasks once we are handling their tedious automations for them, and monitoring them as well.

Liam Collopy says, "Digital solutions as a subscription service has certainly made my life much easier because I don't have dependencies on something I have no control over anymore. I didn't have control over my internal IT systems. Now that I have this solution as a service where a service is provided to me, I don't have to worry about the technology anymore."

"It gives us great pleasure to hear the feedback from our customers. They tell us they're able to accomplish tasks much more efficiently, as well as provide better value with the different functions they play in their organizations," Liam said. "There's peace of mind in knowing that they have the support when they need it. There's a team managing this service for them. There's a technology platform that is available day in and day out in the cloud. They don't have to depend on their own team any longer. They rely on a service."

An oil-and-gas customer originally brought us in to bid on doing a company-wide Windows 10 migration for them. They were going to upgrade their desktops, which is a very basic kind of work in our industry. We were competing against some huge companies, such as Dell, to get the job. We succeeded in changing the discussion to be one of what to do once your desktops have been implemented. That opened the door to the pain they didn't know they had.

They maintain a dedicated staff of people to manage all the subsequent patches themselves, meaning they would have to do them all manually. We were then able to sell them Launch as an automated solution that would roll out to all their desktops, and maintain them for the long term. This would be the last time they ever had to do a desktop migration as we would own it from that point on. This would free those select staff members from being responsible for patch maintenance, enabling them to do other jobs. This customer is an excellent example of doing a leading-edge digital solution for the very old kind of job of upgrading people's desktops.

Apollo's strategy

"If you want something or I'm trying to sell you something, and we're talking, I may have already done all my research on you. I already know all there is to know about you, but I'm not going to come across like that. That's not what you want to hear or see," Apollo says. "I'm going to ask you a bunch of questions. If you're struggling with this particular area in marketing, let's talk a little bit about it. What are some of the things that are causing issues?"

The customer says, "Well, when somebody comes to our website, they click around, and then they end up leaving."

I ask a simple question, "Why do you think that is?"

"Well, we think it's because of X, Y or Z."

I say, "That's interesting because we have other customers with similar problems. One of the reasons they were having those issues was because of these three things."

Then the customer says, "I didn't even think about that. I wonder if that's our problem and I wonder if there's a way for us to be able to overcome that."

Do you see how we just turned this whole thing into them getting solutions? They're solving a problem that we already know how to solve, but we're letting them solve it and come up with the idea. In the end, we say, "That sounds very good. We could help you with that. We can take everything that you just said, and have a couple of our guys and gals take care of that for you. Because that's a good idea, you just nailed it."

"Ultimately," Apollo explains, "the art of the sale is that we don't solve your problems immediately. We ask you some leading questions to help you come up with the idea on your own and then pat you on the back because you did such a good job coming up with what we already knew was the right idea. We already know the answer, but we want you to come up with it on your own."

"The way I'm explaining it all seems very psychological and contrived," Apollo admits. "David didn't create this thing, but he naturally does it without being contrived. That's what makes him special. People like him are very successful at selling. I've been in many meetings with David, and I've seen it happen over and over again. He knows how to bring these things together. If you've never been exposed in the business world to this thing, that's ultimately what it is. It always ends up with you trying to listen to the customer, understand their challenges and their pain, relate to it, and then be able to lead them to the right solution without telling them flat out what it is."

GOING ON YOUR CUSTOMER'S RIDE

The idea behind Spyglass is that every company that's audited from a security perspective — any company that is handling things like credit-card information, socials, customer data and phone numbers — must have data security and compliance. You need to be either ISO-certified or PSI-compliant, and there are several different industry-established types of things that companies need to adhere to if they want to do business.

Spyglass can keep track of all of those compliance issues. If a customer has 100 potential compliance issues, we put those 100 in the system, and as we solve them, we check the box, and we're then able to justify that we're in compliance and that we have a history of the steps we took to be in compliance.

Understanding the why

One of our biggest partners is Microsoft, and for Microsoft to do business with us, we must adhere to certain standards of data security and compliance. They send us a 50-to-100-page document with a list of what we must assess and implement. Then they'll audit us and determine whether or not we did everything according to what they said we needed to do. If we don't meet or exceed the criteria, then Microsoft won't do business with Catapult.

The document has a whole lot of business processes that need to be evaluated or put into effect. For example, one process may be that no one should be able to walk into our building without a badge or security code. The next thing on the list might be a rule that if anyone is away from their computer for more than five minutes, then it needs to auto-lock itself.

Ultimately, the result of viewing that document will expose 100 to 200 things that Catapult needs to do to be in compliance with Microsoft. Of those 200 things, perhaps 100 of them are items related to data security and data compliance that require some level of software, and some sort of process re-engineering kit to address them.

When we look at those 100 items, we know we have to do all 100 of them. What we uncovered was that of these 100, about 90 percent of them can be solved with a few different technologies that are out there, such as everyday best-of-breed security products. For example, Microsoft has something called Enterprise Mobility & Security (EM+S), and that allows you to secure people's phones, their laptops and their iPads. It will also allow you to secure servers and computers, and different tasks you're doing on computers.

EM+S does probably 50 percent of what is listed in that one document from Microsoft. Then there are other software products that we can provide and implement that will solve the rest of the problems. Well, we looked at what we were having to do and figured if we had this problem and this was how we were solving it, how many other companies were feeling the same pain and could use the processes we developed for ourselves.

What we discovered is that a lot of other companies have this same problem (pain) and we saw a huge market. EM+S is one of the most popular software products that Microsoft makes. It's a billion-dollar software product, and it's just getting bigger and bigger. We decided to build some IP, take everything that we'd done for ourselves and for other customers in the past around this area, turn it into a solution as a service and call it data security and compliance as a service, or Spyglass.

We implement all the security technology that you need in data-compliance software because we've already implemented it multiple times, so we already know how to do it quickly.

It's easy for us to go on this ride with our customers because we're already in the same boat. There are different certifications out there that companies can get, such as ISO certification or PCI certification. PCI and ISO are similar security designations, whose purpose is to identify what you're doing as a company to secure your organization and assets. They work to recommend technology that you'll need to secure certain aspects of your company. They want to make sure that you have a process in place for various different types of concerns. That's one aspect of security.

Spyglass is also for customers who don't have to be in compliance with an outside entity. Say you're a midsize company and you don't have these rules but you want to implement your own compliance levels. If your company wants to create your own thing, we're happy to explain the technology that we think will best suit your company, and explain how we will simply take it over for you. Why do you need to hire somebody to manage this aspect of security when we can just do it for you all the time? We're there to support you.

Ask critical questions about the importance of security.

How do you know what your users and employees are doing, and if they're doing the right things at your company? Are they acting responsibly or exposing your company and your customers to risk? How do you handle a disgruntled employee? What is the process to get them out of the building safely and securely and keep your other employees safe? Those are just a couple of examples of internal threats companies may face.

Then you've got external threats such as hackers trying to break into your network, and trying to do more than steal social security numbers. Sometimes they're trying to deny access to whatever it is that you do; if you're an e-commerce company, they might want to bombard your website with so much traffic that nobody else can get to it. What if there's a breach, and somebody hacks into your network? What systems and processes do you have in place that will both identify and remediate that breach?

There's a whole range of things from a security perspective that, if you don't have the right systems in place, will leave you more susceptible to hacking. Over the years, organizations have grown that specialize in evaluating your company to determine how secure you are and what different things you're doing that impact security. What they've discovered is that many companies don't make security a focus. Many of the issues these companies run into from a security perspective are of their own making through inaction.

People who specialize in or understand security and how to keep things secure are hard to find.

Plus, they're pretty expensive. You're probably not going to have a whole team of people, because this is generally quite a high cost depending on the size of the company. Your options are to hire, or buy software and hope it works. Some companies think that if they train their people on the software, they can make it work. Or they can hire a company to do all of it for them. But what happens if it doesn't work?

If you ask any high-ranking IT person today in America if they're worried about breaches of security, if they're being honest, the answer is "Yes". Everyone's concerned about the issue; they're worried about stolen corporate information. People are hearing about foreign hacking and theft of IP. If there's blood moving through their veins, they're concerned and worried about security. They, therefore, have probably bought multiple products, and they've hired numerous people, and there's still a whole lot of praying going on because they know that they're still vulnerable. As soon as they put a solution in place, hackers are looking for ways to breach that solution. It probably will never end.

We come in and say that we'd be interested in taking that issue off your plate.

Our question-and-answer process naturally leads you to understand how we can help you. We have the solutions. Let us worry about it. Hold us accountable. We've created some IP, and we're going to bring a security expert to watch your systems using our IP all the time. We'll report issues, but more importantly, we'll solve them in real time. You'll never have to buy another security product or hire another security expert. Using Spyglass, we'll take care of it.

There are always security threats, so the technology that you use to help identify and remediate threats must always be maturing and evolving as well. In some cases, you don't have much control over who is building the software and what they're focusing on. But I could tell you from our perspective, and as it relates to the service, we've invested in resources that aren't computers but actual people; our security coaches are always on the forefront of anything that could be an issue.

There's an energy company in Houston, Texas that bought our security solution Spyglass, a little less than a year ago. That company decided to go on this journey with us, and on Day 1 after we implemented, they had suspicious-looking activity that our security coach caught. We worked with that customer to overcome that potential security breach and keep that bad guy out. That company estimated that we saved them $300,000 on Day 1 of implementing our solution as a service. We immediately located that breach that was about to take place. They admitted they would never have found it, and they estimated that we saved them about a million dollars in litigation fees. We saved them far more money than the solution will ever cost.

With just one client, that was the result. We were able to take what we learned in that instance and apply it to our entire product. The idea is that hopefully it never happens again. But it actually helped us to build this story now that's very tangible. We can always use that story to explain that here's what our service did for this company and we can do the exact same thing for you.

We always have someone keeping track of what's happening in the market and in the world of security to ensure we're up to date and relevant.

There will always be challenges, and from an innovation perspective, the way we'll mature and evolve is by leveraging technology that can learn faster from things that happen. That gets into AI and deep learning and machine learning where we are looking at large amounts of data from across multiple companies and making recommendations to our customers around things that they need to be watchful of — new threats are coming that you may not have heard of and here's what you need to do to prepare. Or we get information that tells us that there's a potential hack coming that your company could be susceptible to because of your industry.

That's always going to be a challenge, and we must keep up.

We've made the investment in our people to keep track of that, and in the future, that won't be good enough. We'll need help involving AI that will be able to help us predict what can happen at any given moment in time. That's where the market is going as it relates to security and compliance. The question is how to be able to predict when something like that is more likely to happen. In the case of a brute-force attack, there may be signs and warnings. So the question becomes how we can know, and give you some data points that will improve your ability to predict if you're going to experience a breach.

Liam Collopy says, "As far as the subscription-as-a-service model is concerned, there are several reasons why it's beneficial to our security customers. These solutions are highly secure in the Microsoft cloud and are easy to deploy. You can scale up and down as you need to, and they're available anytime, anywhere. We're not restricted by our company systems and infrastructure. It adds that level of flexibility and control over that aspect of my job, whereas before, I was dependent on our IT infrastructure, procedures and policy. Now I'm the one who determines what and when. The technology and complementing services support that now, rather than becoming the hindering factor preventing us from doing our jobs effectively."

These solutions are always improving. New features and functionalities are deployed whenever they're ready, without having to take the system down.

The customers benefit from these services continuing to evolve. One point of interest is that our customers understand that we're going to be continually developing new ways to protect them, and those things are going to be made available to everybody else. Everybody benefits from other clients buying our systems because new functionalities are coming out all the time.

Using the Fuess Method when selling Spyglass to our customers relies heavily on marrying up their why and their pain with our solutions while showing them that more is always possible.

USING THE FUESS METHOD IN THE DIGITAL REALM

Let's say there are some companies out there who don't necessarily see the value of the latest digital trends right away. They don't yet understand their pain. They carry on with business as usual, perhaps subscribing to the "If it ain't broke, don't fix it" way of thinking.

We can still utilize the reasoning behind this old-fashioned method that we're applying to a new digital realm. Say you pick up this book and think, "We're not going to be digitally transforming, so why would this be useful to me?" All you have to do is strip away the digital pieces and find that the method remains the same and applies anywhere and at any time.

Customers come to us for any number of things, and although we're digital-transformation leaders, most of the time they don't come to us specifically for that reason. We've been in business for 25 years, and it's only been the last three or four years that most of the services we provide would fall under a digital-transformation umbrella. Many customers still come to us for the type of things we were doing maybe 10 or 15 years ago; they want old-fashioned, solid, core-development kinds of things.

Naturally, we want to upgrade them to a more current solution set; a digital-transformation solution set. We understand their pain, even if they don't yet, as we were once in their shoes. If someone comes to us for email migration, we might say, "We see your problem. While we can certainly do email migrations, would you like to take a broader look at how communication takes place inside your organization beyond just email?" We might learn they're using Yammer for internal communications, or Skype for conference calls, and they both would be side doors that open to selling Fuse to them.

Selling in the digital realm means you lose some of the benefits of reading body language, measuring tone, and seeing how they present themselves and their image.

With the advent of the digital age, what would previously have been a face-to-face interaction has more or less moved into electronic communication. This shift required reverse engineering of the Fuess Method so technology can enable the same interaction to take place digitally that would have historically been in person. In a face-to-face situation, those are all great things to pay attention to. The list of things to take in on a digital interaction is, however, much longer during your interaction.

For example:

- Determine how to personalize communication/ interaction.
- Look for patterns regarding customer preferences.
- Rank prospects according to their interest.
- Use your website to as a stealth sales tool to start the process.

When having a conversation about a topic or an idea with two separate people, the end result should be identical, which is a movement towards whatever the goal is. The method should be the same as well, but the words and the style would be individually adapted as the two communication styles could be markedly different. That comes easily when you're face to face with a prospect, but in a digital world, you have to figure out how to do the same thing minus the cues.

Naturally, we've had to adapt our communication style, as in the digital world we had to figure out a way to personalize this method of interaction.

It requires adapting the methods that you use to get to know your counterpart by asking some questions and establishing his profile as quickly as possible. One way or another, you have to get a read. You can only ask questions or ask for preferences. One of the benefits of selling in the digital world would be that you could easily ask questions that might be awkward to ask in person. There are things that you would think were very strange if a human was asking you. For example, it would be awkward for me to ask, "How do you like to be communicated to?" You don't find that strange if a computer is asking you because you understand that the computer is trying to get to know you. In person, you expect to get to know each other through talking and visiting.

When personalizing the customer's journey, we have to know who they are and what's important to them.

What do they like? What do they dislike? What are they trying to accomplish? Through a variety of methods — asking questions and understanding responses and categorizing these things using what's called machine-learning — we look for patterns. In some ways, it's become easier to build customer profiles because we can pull out information through a computer that's hard to pull out of a person. People will write it down, but they don't necessarily want to sit and talk about it.

You can build a profile using demographics of various types, but you're having a different kind of interaction with a computer, a web page, with something digital or electronic rather than in person. The method remains the same but the venue changes. With a new venue, you ask questions differently. The Fuess Method can, therefore, be done in person, on the phone or in the digital realm; it just needs to be adapted to the venue.

Selling digitally using digital means

For example, if someone goes to our website, they could be looking at anything. At first, they may be looking for general information about what the solution is, so they get a spec sheet. They travel to the area that describes the benefits of the solution. That's the first level. We have a ranking, a point scale that indicates how warm a prospect is. Until they get to a certain number of points, it doesn't merit any sort of follow up with them because the statistics tell us they're nowhere close to being ready to buy, and if we speak to them now, we may actually turn them off. It's too early to begin talking to them.

We start the journey by collecting personal information to gauge their interest and then track what they do. We use data to tell us about each customer. For them to start the journey, they have to enter in who they are, what company they're with, and what their email address is. For them to receive anything that they ask for, we're going to send it to their email address. They can't receive it if they're lying to us about their email address, for example.

Say they looked at a spec page and then returned and wanted to find out what other customers were using, so they pulled down a case study, that would be worth some additional points. Then say they came back and pulled down a white paper that was talking about the competitive landscape, or maybe the ROI that another customer experienced, that's a third touch in the journey of the customer. Now they may have accumulated enough points for us to consider them a warm prospect. At that point, a salesperson takes a look at the customer's journey.

What did they pull down? When did they do it? Did this person do it three days in a row, or was there a month in between? It tells you her interest level and gauging that is a part of the method. We want to acquire that knowledge as quickly as possible. There may be six or seven steps of various things she can do when they're still a prospect, but it's still working her through the journey towards a sale.

Using your website as a stealth sales method or sales tool

We think of a website as much more than a static informational tool. If somebody's coming to our site, there's a reason why she's doing so. We want to understand the reason. If the reason has to do with intentionally becoming a customer of ours, that's prioritizing the journey, and it's tracked more closely. We don't necessarily need to know that you came to our website to learn what our address is so you can send us a piece of mail. As soon as you come onto the site and you're doing something that indicates you may be interested in learning about some of our solutions, that journey is treated much differently.

Think of your website as the voice of your company. It's the electronic salesperson of your company, which means inherently it has to treat every visitor uniquely just like in a face-to-face sales scenario. It needs to have a very positive interaction with each potential customer. It needs to have purpose, and it needs to be intuitive, smart and attractive.

It needs to have the same characteristics as a human who is interacting with a potential customer.

Way too many companies fall into the trap of having a thoughtless website because everyone is expected to have a website these days. You might think that if someone Googles you and you don't have a site, then you don't even look like a company. But you must consider what you're going to put out there. You actually want to see it as though you're going to put stuff up there that a potential buyer of your services is going to find interesting and attractive. It needs to be done with great thought.

Consider that old adage that you only get one chance to make a first impression. The concept of a journey is a great metaphor to use. If someone's first experience with Catapult is our website, and our site is crummy, they're going to think Catapult's crummy. If they have a negative experience, they're going to believe that Catapult's a negative experience. So all of these things need to be taken into consideration in the digital world.

Your website needs to be intuitive, and a given person's interest should be as easy to find on the site as another's interest, which are going to be two different interests.

A 50/50 mix on your website may be 50 percent being the sales function, yet the magic comes in when visitors don't feel like they're being sold. We recommend that you think of the digital experience of your constituents. Your constituent could be a person in media. It could be a person who wants to buy your services. It could be a prospective new employee of the company. It could be a business partner.

Treat all of those experiences as an opportunity to land your brand and your image, because if it's done positively, it's ultimately going to equate to a top line in your business growth. Whatever mix works best for your individual company is what you should pursue as it's a part of the method itself.

The critical piece of information to take away here is that we all need to think about our digital presence in a different way. There are many tools out there to help you when you're ready. The big question is in what way you need to think of it differently. You might need a professional to help you figure out how you need to think about your site based on your constituents.

UTILIZING THE GROUP FUESS

Think of sports, such as football, soccer and golf. The discipline and anticipation associated with these sports are embodied by being able to think at least a couple of moves in advance of what's going to happen. In hockey, they say, "Go where the puck is going to be, not where it is." The anticipation — being two or three moves ahead — puts you in a prepared position for what does happen.

There's another concept crucial to team sports — people on successful teams typically play for their teammates before they play for themselves. If you tune in to the end of the championship series and listen to an interview, you'll typically hear them say, "All the credit goes to my teammates. The reason I show up every day and work so hard is for my teammates." Now, it's very easy to think that just sounds good, but it's actually true. The best individuals on the best teams aren't playing for themselves first. They're playing for their teammates. There's an undeniable inspirational cumulative effect with a group of people working together that creates a 1+1=3 situation.

At Catapult Systems, we hold offsite year-end executive strategy meetings every November at an Austin resort where our ten most essential executives from across the company gather to talk about the business. It's a very tedious look at our business, and we hit it as though it's the first time we've ever hit it. As the leader of the company, naturally, I'm always questioning how we can grow more, increase our margins, and examine the best ways to grow, as well as questioning what the cost would be to develop in specific directions.

While I was preparing for one particular meeting, an idea came to me around a new way of growing. Historically, every time we wanted to open up a new market across the United States, we got together as a group and decided it was time to open up a new market. Then we decided where we wanted to do it — in the eastern, western or central United States. Then we went through a process of elimination while allowing a few locations to bubble up to the surface.

Let's say we decided on the West, for example, and next, we suggested that Denver, Portland, Salt Lake City and Seattle are all decent cities. Then we narrowed it down to one. That was our previous method of growth in creating a new physical geography. It was the only way we had ever grown; the only muscle we had ever flexed. At some point, it became less efficient for our growth, as there were new ways to look at it.

Opening a new office is quite expensive. Each of our new offices tends to run us about a million dollars before we get into the black and start to break even. There's usually a three-year payback on opening a new office before we pay ourselves back that million dollars and begin to make money. It's a long road to recoup our original investment.

The offices are very dependent on people, so I had to find a leader for each of those offices every time we started one. The success and the failure of that office would almost always ride along with the leader, so if we made a poor choice, we set ourselves back a year or two, depending on how quickly we took action. Then it was dependent on hiring a team of salespeople, a team of delivery consultants and so forth. Each of those people only served that market. Say we opened an office in Denver and hired 20 people to get to a critical-mass size, and over time, we would need many more than that. Those people only served that marketplace. Then we had to redo that in other geographic areas each time we opened a new office.

I wondered if there was a better way to grow and serve new markets. One night, I was alone with my head in my hands in a dark room. An idea came to me about how I could get economies of scale where we did it once in a centralized location and then sold everywhere and de-livered everywhere. How would that impact our existing model? As you can imagine, I spent many hours without answering all these questions. After all, I had to take my-self through the Fuess Method, didn't I?

It's important to add into the method that you don't actu-ally need to — nor should you be — trying to see around every corner, and to answer every question in preparation for visiting with a potential audience. You need to allow for creative wiggle room in those gray areas and leave some intentional gaps that can be filled in by the audi-ence when they fall in love with their own ideas. You can take those gaps and expand upon them as often and as long as needed until they've bought into their own ideas. That's an important little tidbit to the method.

At our retreat, we had ten executives sitting in a confer-ence room, and the question on the table was what we were going to do this coming year concerning growth. Imagine me standing at a whiteboard with the usual first question I had for the group. But this time I said that I'd like to take a different approach to the question we have every year, which usually is "Is it time to start a new office and where should it be?" This time I said, "Let's think differently this year and start at the top. What are some of the gotchas associated with growing the way we've been growing?"

Next, I established a sandbox of the problem set. I said, "I don't know that we're going to come up with a solution to this problem." This is quite a crafty technique because I was saying they didn't have to come up with the answer. Instead, I relied on them to work with me and come up with the solution — and it's a "we" thing. I said, "I'm not sure we're going to come up with a great answer to this problem set, but it clearly is a problem." In this case, I didn't have to find or sell the pain. Everyone in the room was already aware of the problems and expenses of opening a new office.

In similar scenarios, most of the time, the idea would be the one I was trying to sell anyway, but the group thought it was theirs. That was why the sale of my concept or idea had a very high likelihood of taking place. Even if it wasn't my idea, and someone came up with a better one, the concept or idea still was sold because the end state that I was trying to achieve was solving a problem without solving it for them. They were going to execute on it, and I didn't have to baby it along. What I did, in this case, was help my executives go down a path with the idea that they were going to come up with a solution together, or maybe not.

The "or maybe not" is important. I took the pressure off at the beginning of the meeting by saying, "We may not come up with the answer." This immediately freed their creativity because they didn't feel like they were on the spot to solve a problem. They didn't need to be defensive in thinking, "Fuess is going up to the whiteboard. He's going to sell us this big idea, and then, once he tells us what it is, we have to agree. Then he's going to go back and get the box of T-shirts he's already had made and pass them out." I didn't want them to feel that way, naturally. It wasn't certain that they were going to come up with a solution, but they were going to go on that journey together. The pressure was off to allow for creativity.

When I asked for the challenges associated with opening a new geographical location, I received a dozen answers, including:

- It's very expensive.
- The payback takes a long time.
- If you make a mistake, you get set back a long time.
- You can't open more than one or two at a time because it's so expensive.

I agreed that all of those challenges the team identified were true, yet at the same time, they all had a desire to grow at a faster pace and do it profitably. They all knew how they had done it in the past, so I asked them to set that aside for a moment and establish what the criteria would be for doing it differently. Instead of talking about what the approach was going to be, I backed them over to talk about what the criteria for a successful new approach would look like. Now, that's an example of a question you can ask 50 different ways, but the point I want you to take away is that I only moved ahead one step. I could have jumped ahead to "Let's talk about an idea I have for doing this differently." That would have been like going from A to Z, and nobody would get brought along on that leap.

Instead, I facilitated a group discussion and asked them questions about what their problem sets were. I asked what they saw as the different things at play; the different guide rails; the things that surrounded the issues that they were dealing with in coming up with potential solutions.

Now, I had already come up with the idea to create a national sales team and delivery team that sold everywhere except in the markets covered by our existing offices. I was faced with having to sell this idea to the group. I already knew what I felt was the best solution because I had thought it through. I was open to improving upon this idea, or even changing it if someone presented a better one. I planned to lead them through a process where they came up with the answer together, and it would be the exact same answer that I had from the outset.

I could have just walked in and told them what we were going to do. That's what many people do in sales. Disappointingly, many leaders just walk in and say, "This is what we're going to do." Well, you don't have any buy-in from anybody when you do it that way, as they didn't get to participate in the process of thinking of and arriving at that solution. Again, even with your staff, you want solutions to be their ideas because that's how you're going to get the best out of them.

I already knew what I felt was going to be the right answer, but I didn't want to impose my idea on the group, because if I could get the entire group to think it was their idea, then it was sold. The premise that I always operate on when I'm selling is if I can get you to see the problem and the solution, and you own the solution, then it's your idea, and we're golden. I'll never take credit for it, and that's the ego thing because, for this methodology to be effective, I have to be able to set my ego aside. If I can't set it aside, then this method is clearly not the right one for me.

The team talked about their problem set, and about the criteria they might use to bounce new possibilities off the wall. They ended up with a big whiteboard filled with creative thinking ideas:

- We need to grow at a less-expensive rate.
- We need to be able to scale.
- We need to be able to open more than one area at a time.
- We need to be less dependent on finding multiple teams across the country.

Then they took another step and brainstormed on potential ways to solve the problem. At that point, I said, "In listening to you guys, I have a picture in mind. It describes this sandbox that we've created here. Here are our offices," and I drew a freehand picture of the United States. I drew circles around the markets that we served, centered on eight cities. I drew a little circle around each city, and asked, "What do you see here?"

They said, "Well, that's a picture of Catapult and the markets we serve."

"Right. What else do you see?"

"A lot of white space, and a lot of areas that we don't serve in the United States."

"Yep! Exactly. So, what do you think the GDP is of the markets that we serve relative to the whole of the United States?"

They were looking at the seven or eight cities with little circles around them and the massive amounts of white space. My question to them was around how much of the United States we were serving using the model that we had. Some light bulbs started coming on, and looking back on it, it seems simplistic, but it was our world at the time. We batted it around, and the answer was that we were only serving 5 percent of the GDP of the United States.

I said, "Fine. Let's go with that. It doesn't matter whether it's five or seven or three. It's small." I got group agreement around that fact. "The question is then if we want to sell our business, and we want to get some fast growth in, and we don't want to spend as much money as it historically takes because we don't have that kind of time, what methods we could use to do so."

I didn't come up with any solutions. I just asked questions. I had to be careful how leading my questions were, because the more leading questions like this are, the more people start to feel they're being walked down a path and they don't like that. You have to ask questions that allow people to use their brains, and that's where the art is in this method. It's natural and universal for aggressive salespeople to go right to the answer, or ask extremely leading questions, which can offend intelligent people. Often they shut down at that point. You must allow people to come up with the answer themselves.

The beauty of this method is when they come up with the solution, smart people — and remember I said one of the core requirements is that you're dealing with rational, intelligent people — who are asked well-tailored questions that aren't offensive will allow their own light bulbs to shine. It'll be the right answer most of the time, and the one you were trying to get them to, but the approach is what sells them because they sold themselves.

I asked my team, "What are some ways we can serve the rest of the country to get fast growth? Let's just brainstorm on some ways that we can serve the rest of the country without creating an office in New York City, which doesn't help solve the problem. We're now only serving a further two or three more percentage points of the GDP." We got a brainstorming session going on ways to solve our problem, and at that point I had them. That was a way of illustrating "Here's where we are in this walk down the yellow brick road and here's why we're walking down the yellow brick road together."

The team walked themselves straight into the intended outcome. It's not a trap — because it's not a bad game. This method isn't something where they walk away and feel like they lost. It has to be a win for them, and sometimes buying a house is a win, and sometimes buying a car is a win, and sometimes changing the sales and delivery model is a win, but I had my team at that point because I had them thinking about a problem.

They started going off on tangents of how to fund new offices. At that point, nobody had come up with the national concept yet, so I took a few of their ideas and glued them together. Naturally, if you get a group of people who have been in the business a long time, they know the parameters, the positives, the negatives and the guide rails associated with it. I had the luxury of having spent much more time thinking about this problem. This was the first time they were thinking about it.

Then when we brainstormed on it, inevitably one of the ideas that they came up with — because I got to participate in the brainstorming — was the idea that I had. Occasionally, in situations like this, an even better idea comes up, which is great, because ultimately we're all trying to solve the problem. You have to be able to be egoless, and go with the best idea if this happens. Remember the importance of being egoless? If the team decided on my idea that I walked in with, that would be great, and if it were a better idea from someone else, that would be great too. The idea is to get the solution to a problem, and that's the most important thing.

We brainstormed, and I stayed in the questioning mode of "So if we took this path, how much would it cost us? What do we think would be the result of it?" Maybe we had seven or eight ideas, and then because it's a rational, smart group of people, we started zeroing in on the top ideas. I knew what a robust solution would be, so I started guiding the conversation, yet allowed it to be theirs. I tried to get as many of the ideas as possible so that it touched everybody in the room and started gluing them together one by one.

I got people thinking and putting the puzzle together. "You take this piece of the idea, and you glue it in here, and now what do we have? We have this, and we have that, and we have this, and it's incrementally better than what we've ever done." With each of those pieces added to it, each of them is thinking, "Well, that's it." We came up with the idea together. Slowly, I painted a picture using their ideas, by gluing more and more of them together, and then we had something that probably still fell short of the new idea or new concept. If it doesn't fall short, and it nails the whole thing, you're finished. Now you can rally around it.

The critical part of the process is that they were building something together using my questions as opposed to "Let me tell you the answer that I've come up with in the back room." They were all buying into it at that point, and they were thinking, and their light bulbs were going off, and there was all this creativity going on in the room. Then I asked if we did these five things that all came up in the room, how we could do that once and have that benefit the 95 percent of the GDP opportunity in the United States that we're not addressing today.

I got the natural pause. Then someone said, "What if we created a centralized team here in Austin and their territory was the 95 percent space out there?" And someone else said, "That's a great idea. We could have one general manager and one sales team and divide them up by East, Central and West. Then they'll be a traveling group as opposed to everybody staying local in their market. We'd have the delivery resources in Austin, Texas and have them all travel as well. They can borrow people from one office to deliver in another."

This idea started building upon itself, and I did nothing except ask questions to get the exact result that I was anticipating. Usually — and this is important — you'll get a better answer because you took 10 smart people and walked them down the yellow brick road. You take 10 intelligent people chewing on an idea and robustly discussing it, and almost every time you'll get a better buildout than what the straw man came up with in the back room.

This is why it's essential to leave white space in your ideas. You don't need to build these things all the way out and run spreadsheets against them. Leave plenty of white space for the group to sell themselves. One of the biggest mistakes people in sales can make is when you feel you have to provide all of the answers. If all of the answers are from you, and your only job is to get them to buy all of your answers, that's the opposite of the Fuess Method.

The icing on the cake with this method is the 'accurate assumption'. Let's assume that by using this method and by the end of a session — whether it's an hour or six hours — everyone bought in. There can be a tendency to give this project to one person, and in my case, that would tend to be me as the CEO. If it were a big enough project, I would run this project. Well, there's a more effective way to do it, and that's that I will participate in it but not lead it. I'd like someone to volunteer to run it, and I'd like everybody to take part in it.

What that does is to make sure that the audience fully bought in because they're building it themselves, rather than thinking that it was my idea, and they're required to participate in some way. As a member of the team, I can make sure it's guided correctly and doesn't fall into a ditch; I can keep everyone invested while keeping the project on track.

The result of that scenario was that they created a national sales team that's still in existence today. We now serve every single zip code in the United States and have customers in almost every American state, including Alaska. Our new approach is producing tens of millions of dollars for Catapult Systems' bottom line. Nobody on the team thinks, "Oh, that was David's idea." Individually, they know they all had a part in it, which is why it works, and never to this day have I stood in front of the group and said, "Hey, you know that national sales model that we're using now? Well, that was really my idea." (Oops! I gave it away!)

I never said that and I never will, but Sam Goodner, my ex-business partner, recognized it because Sam's one of those brilliant guys. He's had it done to him so many times where he walked away thinking it was his idea only to have a chance to reflect on it and realize he'd been Fuessed — and it was good for him. To be successful with this method, you can't be malicious or crooked. You have to want genuinely what's best so everybody can win. You can't go back afterward and take credit for it; you have to leave the credit alone.

ADJUSTING FOR SLOW OR FAST DECISION-MAKERS

The Fuess Method can be applied to both slow and fast decision-makers. As a rule, as fast as a sale can be made, it's better that you take it just a hair slower than it could go. That doesn't mean weeks or months. It means that absorption time is appreciated by the person who's buying. It's a small subliminal point, and fast or slow can be defined in a lot of different ways, but slowing it down just a hair more than the buyer wants can work to the seller's advantage.

Give your buyer that little extra bit of absorption time.

If you've done an excellent job, and you're covering their needs and giving a solution to them, it's not as though they're likely to find a better solution in the next two or three days. But they're going to appreciate that you haven't put pressure on them and they'll come back ready to buy in, having made the decision themselves. You end up with an even more committed customer who's more appreciative of your approach because nobody else takes that approach and you still end up with the sale.

If you have an impulsive buyer who won't be persuaded to pause, then that works to your advantage because you can still make that sale. If somebody walks in and says, "I'm buying, and I'm buying right now. I don't care what you say. I'm not leaving here without signing." Do you let them sign? Of course, you do. That's not the norm, though.

Respect the natural progression to making a sale.

The buyer and seller generally know when they're sitting at the table and it's buy time. Both parties know, and when it's buy time, you should give him that extra moment to take a breath, pause and consider. You can call it reconsider, but if you've done an excellent job up to that point, he's not going to find something else in a short period of time. He's just not. Your job is to give him that opportunity to pause, and he will come back even more committed to what you are selling.

If a customer is slow about making a decision, that's quite common. Your job is to progress the sales cycle along, and that takes some creative methods of finding out what's preventing him from making a decision without putting too much pressure on him. Something is stopping him, whether it's a lack of information or not knowing if he can get the support from his boss. You should uncover whatever is preventing him from making a decision. Once that obstacle has been removed, you move into the same approach just mentioned. You ruthlessly remove barriers that slow down the cycle, and when you get to buy time, you ease off on the pressure and let him recommit himself to the sale.

What we sell at Catapult is considered a complex sale. Some things are deemed simple transactions, such as which brand you're going to buy at the grocery store. You're going to make that determination quite quickly. The more expensive a transaction it is, the more complex the sale. You look for little wins that are going to add up over time to get you to a place where you can end up in a buying situation. In what we're selling, it's a multi-touch sale, so each time we leave a meeting, we're looking for the open door to have a subsequent discussion, assuming it was an inappropriate time to make that sale at that time.

Never let a sale reach a yes/no decision no matter what speed decision-maker you're dealing with.

You should always ask open-ended questions versus yes/no questions, as having an open-ended sales cycle is always preferable to a closed-ended sales cycle that's a yes/no. You leave an opening for a subsequent discussion or something of meaning for me to come back to you with when you aren't at yes/no. That's the key. You want to assess at each meeting, at each phase, if there's a potential sale at hand. If so, you need to implement the method just mentioned, which is to leave an opening for a subsequent discussion.

At one executive meeting, I pointed out that we had a lot of opportunities in the pipeline at 60 percent and 80 percent which were close, but the customer hadn't signed the contract. I brought the team together and showed how much revenue Catapult could potentially be looking at that was sitting at 80 percent. I asked the group why they were still at 80 percent. Everybody was able to articulate the why, although, as in just about any case, the individual team members arrived at their conclusions at varying speeds. Then as a team, with me leading them, I helped bring everybody to the same page and the same speed as it related to "If this is why it's happening and we're sitting at 80 percent, then let's come up with a solution together." Then after presenting the pain, I wanted everyone in the room to agree to the solution.

If the team couldn't agree, then they would have to figure out what they needed to do to get there, and then execute on what they had agreed to. This could have been a challenging situation as it related to the need for the team to get on the same page at somewhat similar speeds, come up with solutions, and then execute. They had to hold themselves accountable for what they had proposed every week. They had to make sure that they did what they said they were going to do with these five clients and then report to the group on how things went. They talked about that every single week so that they could get things pushed over the line. Eventually, by pulling as a team, they were able to solve those particular challenges, and methods like that are what keep the Catapult engine humming.

PROVIDING NEW VALUE TO EXISTING CUSTOMERS

There are three selling scenarios we set out to cover in this book, and we have now covered selling to an internal audience and selling outside of your company to your customers. Now we will discuss approaching a sale concerning the benefit of selling to the customers of your customers. Selling to your customer's customer is technically selling to your customer, but doing it in a way that focuses on the value that they can deliver to their customers.

The magic is when you apply my unique method to the technology companies use, you're helping the customers learn a very effective way of selling to their customers. Technology is just enabling it. It's getting them to take action, and as long as they're taking action, we can help them. When there's no action, that's when you can't help.

When you consider social media, such as Facebook or Twitter, many use these platforms to reach customers. It could be said, therefore, that Facebook and Twitter sell to the customers of their customers. We could name a dozen other tools. They can all be effectively used, depending on what you're trying to achieve with your customer and the demographics of your customer, and what exactly it is you're trying to convince them of with that product or service. Those are indeed options, and your case may be the perfect options. They also may not be the ideal options. We need to explore together what are the right places for you to get your message across.

In our business and industry, we're typically building custom software for companies to use internally; that is to automate processes or to integrate systems, but they're mostly behind the scenes. They might have an interface to an end user, but most are very much internal. There are customers, however, with which we're building something that's going to interface directly with our customer's customer. One scenario is selling to a chief marketing officer or vice president of HR. Once you're in, then your services must be sold internally to their employees, because if they don't buy in, then you don't have a sale from that officer or vice president.

A good example of selling to our customer's customer is one of our clients that we will call Main Street Bank. It's quite a large regional bank, and they found themselves beginning to compete with many nimble, smaller community banks that were becoming more and more automated. Main Street is a bigger, more traditional bank and has more legacy systems. Customers tend to walk into Main Street and do all of their interactions with a teller.

Our audience, in this case, isn't Main Street, but their customers. Main Street wanted to go digital to appeal to a younger audience, which is common with most of the major banks today. We had to learn what was appealing to the audience of the bank; what features they wanted to see; how they wanted to interact with the bank electronically; what kind of experience they wanted to have when they walked into a bank.

We did a lot of analysis by physically sitting in a bank and watching the interactions taking place, doing surveys with customers, and doing a competitive analysis on areas in which we could leapfrog the competition. Younger audiences usually do their banking from home. That's the wave of the future. So when we designed a platform for Main Street, we had to keep in mind how their customers were going to want to interact with the bank.

We added aspects based on observing and interacting with Main Street's customers. If you go into Main Street Bank today, or to their website, you'll see a completely transformed customer experience. The website has an entirely new customer journey and interface. The experience of going into a bank is faster, more streamlined, and more technically appealing. You can conduct your entire banking experience without ever talking to a teller.

You can do it online. There are many reasons why people might prefer to do that. It could be that there's a long line. It could be that they have three or four things they need to get done, and they can do it faster without interacting with a teller. It could be that they're part of a younger audience that prefers not to interact with a human, and would instead do it all through technology.

If you go back to the method of having it be the customer's idea, and never taking credit for it, and essentially letting him sell himself — there's a subliminal sales process taking place every time someone has an interaction with that bank that's intended to make the bank stand out from its competition because it's self-service. Virtually any service that you're interested in can be served up in the way that you're interested in interacting with it. That's applying the method rather than saying, "Here's the way that you can interact with me." Instead, it's saying, "How would you like to interact with me?"

One of the neighborly components of having a community bank is that you get to know your banker and your teller. When you put the automation and computerization into it, you can lose that personal interaction. We wanted to make sure we didn't lose it, but make the banking experience even more personalized than when dealing with a teller. Tellers are going to turn over occasionally. They're going to have good days and bad days. Every time you interact with Main Street Bank — either by using a computer or walking into the bank but using their kiosk — we're making it even more personalized than we could with a teller. Because the teller isn't going to remember or know what you did the last five times you came into the bank. A computer can, and it's relatively easy.

The computer sees patterns, such as you come in every two weeks to deposit a check, you come in once every six months to order new checks, you come in on the quarter to deposit a bonus, and you come in every once a while to withdraw $100 cash to pay for the cleaning service. All of the patterns are captured, and when you walk in, you're not starting from scratch every time with a teller. You choose what you'd like to do and enter your code to identify yourself. More than greeting you by name, the computer can ask questions like "Are you here to reorder checks?" or "As a reminder, your maid service will be there on Monday afternoon. Remember to take out $100 to pay them."

It recognizes all of the patterns of your banking journey, and your journey with Main Street too because they're very different journeys. We each use the bank in entirely different ways, even though it's still putting money in and taking money out at the end, but we have very different patterns on how we bank. For us to know what those patterns are, and serve them up to you, it gets to a point where you would prefer to use the computer rather than interact in person.

The other side benefit is that it can offer credit cards. It can offer memberships to vacations spots. It can advertise if you want to add that element to it based on demographic information or the type of things that you spend money on. There are endless possibilities that Main Street can use that data for.

TAKING CARE OF YOUR EMPLOYEES

Naturally, we use our own systems at Catapult to engage our employees. Before we implemented Fuse, the leaders of our company that help run even our day-to-day operations were feeling that pain so familiar to our customers. There was an inability to find information quickly or to be able to collaborate effectively between different executives and their direct reports. It wasn't bad, but it wasn't scalable, and it wasn't growing based on the needs of our business.

There was poor collaboration and experience. Our intranet wasn't adapting to the way our business was changing and to the habits of not only our customers but also our new employees. Ten years ago, what we had was fantastic, but then we got a whole different set of employees that don't operate the way they did a couple of years ago. Social networking and the ability to be more social with devices and computers didn't exist.

Now, not only is this the way that they want to work, it was the only way they knew how to work. We didn't have systems in place to help them get what they wanted. So they were often left alone in trying to figure things out, and that made them very inefficient and ineffective, which ultimately hurt that employee experience that we so desperately prided ourselves on.

Catapult has been recognized multiple times for being one of the top places to work in the state of Texas, in Central Texas, and in Austin — and has won the *Austin Business Journal*'s Best Places to Work in Central Texas award for four years in a row at the time of this publication. We value our culture, and when our cultural aspect took a hit, our executive team realized we had to make a change. We had to do something very different to help our employees do what they needed to do.

We came up with this concept to think of intranet as a service. We had this need, and we wanted to move in this direction, and it all came together at the right time. We knew we had to make a change in those areas and we also knew we were going to start moving into some new areas to help drive a fresh way of engaging our customers and driving revenue from a subscription-based model. That was important and was one of those pivotal moments where we knew we needed to make a change, we wanted to change, and we wanted to do these things together.

Another thing that brought the group together was cloud computing. While cloud computing has been around since the mainframe computing of the 1950s, it wasn't really big yet. We were thinking through our solution strategy and solutions as a service. But the cloud was really important and our No. 1 technology partner, Microsoft, was betting on having their company on the cloud. Not classic cloud, but developing services that companies can use on a consumption basis.

Their model was to build all these services, and you get to use them and pay for what you use, just like electricity. We said we should think about aligning ourselves to a model that also allows us to consume in that way. Up to that point, the way that we did everything internally at Catapult was if we needed to buy software or we needed to buy hardware, we would have to make those large purchases and then amortize that over time, just like our customers. We understood that pain.

As consumption-based pricing started to emerge, we proposed that instead of paying $100,000 this month, we spread that across 12 months or two years. That would allow us to do more but also get a lot of value. This gave us the ability to get email and several other services that Microsoft provided per user per month. That model really helped us to think through how we wanted to buy, and we saw momentum in the market on buying that way. Then we wondered if we could create a model where our solutions could be sold. We provide a little bit of IP and services, and they pay monthly. We incur more of the risk, but the client incurs less risk. Because we'd benefited from that model, we started thinking about offering it to our customers.

When we started digging into the details, it became more complicated because a lot of our executives run PNLs (profit and loss). They were responsible for their region, or what we called business units. So if we were to go to this new model, what would these new solutions and new technology mean for them? We had guys that were doing some of this older stuff. We decided not to create something so new that it alienated our existing employees. And for the ones for whom this new direction isn't what they're used to, let's get them trained and figure out what we need to do to help them be successful in this new world.

That conversation agreement between the executives and me helped foster an environment of trust where we were not going to move into a new direction that ultimately was going to alienate our guys who had been loyal to us for a long time. We wanted to come up with a model in which the solutions that we build leveraged a lot of the technologies that they're already used to using. But the way we sell it, implement it, price it, and service it would be a little different. It wasn't going to be so huge that you have to adapt radically or want to leave Catapult. Because again, remember culture; we want to keep our employees.

Another thing that the executive team realized as we pitched it to them was that we were very inclusive of the group. We followed the five principles of getting people on the same page when it comes to digital transformation. One way is going to be having a culture of inclusivity of the executive team and the closest people that they work with and trust.

Instead of saying, "This is what we're going to do and we don't care what you say, this is the direction that we're going to go in", we presented what we knew from our own company. We presented what we'd heard from other companies and from technology-platform providers that are driving the future of technology.

"The entire executive team was able to be participants in forming and shaping what this ultimately has become — and it continues to grow and mature," Apollo says. "Being inclusive with the leadership was key in establishing necessary goals and metrics; this roadmap enabled the executive team to look at it and say if we transform our business that way and execute according to what we have all agreed to, then we can expect significant growth and open up new channels of opportunity for Catapult that we've never had access to before. That ultimately sealed the deal in selling to our employees."

SELLING CUSTOMER SERVICE TO YOUR CUSTOMERS

There are some significant challenges that sales and marketing have to deal with on a regular basis. One of those challenges is integration. Often the marketing team thinks that they can do what the sales team does, and the sales team often thinks they can do what the marketing team does. While there's a bit of a tight correlation between the two regarding what they do, they're different functional groups within an organization.

As a corporate business function, marketing is responsible for the messaging that they want customers to see as it relates to the company. They don't just want to put content out there; they want to drive. If you're focused on making money, then you have an end customer. Your marketing job is to articulate what it is that the company does, why it matters, what's the value, and then put different campaigns in place to drive that activity.

Once that activity occurs, then hopefully at some point in the process, that target turns into an actual buying customer. You see this happen all the time. You're on the web, and you see something. Maybe it's an email or an ad, and you're thinking, "That seems pretty good. I want to check that out." When you click on that and go to the company's website, you get to learn more about what it is, and then you determine if you think you want to buy it. You could become a customer. That's the whole marketing attribution part. Marketing does that front-end piece, gets the lead, and fills the funnel with people.

The sales function reaches into the bucket or the funnel and interacts with the hottest leads, with people who seem to want to buy something. Then they try to create a deeper relationship. There's a difference between marketing and sales, but often, the two think that they're stepping on each other's toes. There's friction there, and that friction doesn't do anything to benefit the customer. How can we help them to bridge that gap? That's one thing. The second thing is market share or the many different channels that they use to reach customers. That could be email, a website, mobile ads and apps, or it could be social.

There are just a few channels that make the real impact, and those are the primary ones used to reach potential customers. It's a lot to deal with. Because there's so much variety, even within those few categories, it's hard for marketing departments to target the right customer and capture the data in a way that they can use to drive sales for the salespeople, so that's another challenge.

Marketers and salespeople always want access to the most relevant information to do their respective jobs. They want the data when they need it, and that data changes often. They can't possibly create that reporting for themselves, as they don't necessarily have the people to do that. Salespeople sell, marketing people market. If they need a bunch of customization to reports and dashboards, they have to lean on IT for that, but IT is often busy with other things. That it makes it hard for marketing and sales to get what they need when they need it and remember, they're usually time-sensitive needs.

That's another challenge. You take all of those things together, and you recognize all the complicated stuff that these two groups have to deal with — and that the individual who suffers the most is the end customer. Maybe you see a campaign with some offer. You click on it, but then you're taken to a faulty website or perhaps the site doesn't work well or maybe the messaging on the website doesn't match up with what's in the email. Even if the email campaign and website are working well, once you make it to the salesperson, maybe the messaging is so mixed up that a salesperson is trying to sell you something that isn't what you initially thought you were buying.

As a solution consulting company, we thought we could implement and manage and configure and customize the digital channels, primarily the content management channels like .com. Content management systems do more than just .com, they also do your mobile. They also can help you do things like push information and tidbits out to different social channels. If you go to Twitter and see something and click on it and it takes you to the website, that website captures the source of the activity and then that activity is essential for you to decide whether or not campaigns are effective.

The challenge is that those digital channels, marketing technology, offline/online marketing, and sales execution are all disconnected from the customer. When you add any disconnected marketing, it shows us that harmony doesn't exist between the marketing and sales. So we created our solution, which is a service that delivers an integrated suite of existing sales and marketing technologies combined with a dedicated technologist to enable the harmonious execution of your sales marketing and customer experience and goals.

We take all those external entities from those various channels and bring them together to give marketing and sales the information they need to improve how they reach and interact with the customer. This results in better customer service and experience.

You get a dedicated sales/marketing technology team and you get a continually improved and integrated sales/marketing content-management platform. Companies that come to mind for doing this type of work are Kentico and Sitecore, which specialize in this work. Their content management system, which is basically what customers see, allows you to do so many things, one of which is to help define the customer journey.

Say you go to the Crocs website and you want to interact and buy a pair of shoes. When you're at their website for the first time, it doesn't know who you are. You click around and eventually, you click on the pink Crocs for ladies and then you leave. You come back two days later and that website forgot what you did. If you're interested in buying Crocs, you have to go through the whole process all over again.

Customer experience as a service is when you go back to the Crocs website the second time and not only do you see pink Crocs as the first thing that pops up, but there's a 15 percent discount attached to it. The content management system takes note of the customer's behavior and offers an incentive to try to keep that engagement.

With Agile Analytics, we bring it all together and integrate those three systems — the marketing system, the sales system and the external content management.

We bring all that together, and then we provide you with the insights that you need to have a positive impact on the customer and help the customer either buy your service or register for a webinar or whatever you're trying to get them to do. This is the service with which we do that and the mechanism with which we determine whether or not it was successful. We set up all that technology, configure it, manage it, integrate into what we need it to integrate into so that we can give you the insights necessary to make better business decisions that ultimately impact your buying customer.

In this example, you've got marketing campaigns, created in a marketing or sales system. You put in things like cost and what channels you want it to go out to and determine how the email needs to read, what it needs to look like on social media, and which social channels it needs to go on.

The campaign also has a multi-step process to it. The email goes out, somebody clicks on the email, and they go to a micro-site that has information about an event. After you attend the event, if you've shown interest in the event, we reach out to you. Then you fall into what's called a nurture campaign. So one campaign can lead to another campaign. All of this stuff requires technology to make it all happen seamlessly.

When you're a marketing and sales team, you do this for a living, and what we'll do is support all that. We'll provide the alignment from both a marketing-technology perspective and a sales-technology perspective and make sure there's a consistent customer journey across digital channels because we're going to be the ones managing all the technology.

Customer experience as a service is about helping the customer's customer.

We help our customers improve how they interact and reach their customers so that they can benefit from an end result, whether it's buying a product or attending a conference. We have the technology to help them do that efficiently while continuously improving all the time. You need somebody there to help you from a technology perspective to get the most out of your technology investments.

We're doing some very interesting things with the data that we're getting from all those different places. We can do everything mentioned above in a way that's relevant and specific to your business. While we may not know *your* particular business, we've been in business long enough that we know from a process-automation perspective how to understand enough to make what you're trying to do with the technology more impactful.

We provide the ongoing service and support. The customer is the business stakeholder, so it's their responsibility to determine what strategies they want, and then we make sure that the technology will do what they want it to do. We provide the tools and the know-how to implement it, while they provide their specific ideas for their industry and what they're trying to accomplish.

A good example is a campaign. We don't specialize in campaigns, but say a customer does. They know what campaigns they want, but they need help with "How do I do A/B testing with this particular platform? If I do a campaign and I know I'm automatically going to need to do A/B testing, can you help me set that up from a technology perspective?"

Of course, we can. Because they can't do it themselves, we'll help them. Then we'll learn their business, and we can partner with them until, eventually — although we may not be a campaign company or do campaigns for a living — we'll know enough about their business and how campaigns work that we can be very effective. So that's a crucial element. Think of it as a Trojan-horse strategy by which the more we do for our customer, the more ingrained we get and the more valuable we become.

We leverage analytics and integration to help you gain insights into what you're trying to do, and in this case, it's the customer. How can I impact a customer's behavior? It relates back to the Fuess Method of asking the right questions to get someone to take action for himself and to sell himself on the next step.

USING THE FUESS METHOD IN YOUR PERSONAL LIFE

One of the benefits of learning this method is that virtually all of it can be applied in your personal life, and not just when buying services or products. The technique works equally well in everyday situations. Fundamentally, the Fuess Method is about human behavior and the human condition, which makes it an ideal human method, as opposed to an inanimate method.

For example, you can use the method when deciding on which restaurant you're going to choose for dinner with your spouse or significant other, or when making any decision together that involves more than one person. It's about listening and persuasion by allowing the other person to have the idea, even though it might actually be your own. It's all about interpersonal skills and persuasion, but at a very artful level. It's an elegant way to make decisions between people.

The same thing applies to your personal life, just like it does to your business life. The seller has to start off with a point of flexibility; it can't be 'my way or the highway'. You genuinely want what's best for the customer in a business scenario, and in your personal life, you genuinely want what's best for both parties. In some cases, when you want what's best for the other person, you're willing to sacrifice what you want today because it's the right thing to do. It puts some credits in the 'bank account'.

Other examples of using the ask-and-answer approach indicative of the Fuess Method might be helping your children work through their own decisions. Or getting your way at the next HOA meeting when interacting with neighbors. Negotiating with salespeople of all types — including realtors and car salespeople — becomes much easier when you understand and use the methods described in this book.

This is a very persuasive method. If you're going to be around someone for the next 10 or 20 years, you don't want to sacrifice or taint the relationship. Even when the Fuess Method was being used on Sam, he recognized it and gave it a name when he saw it was happening. There was no reason for him to have negative feelings towards it because all it was doing was allowing him to act on something that he thought was his idea in the first place.

A perfect example of the Fuess Method from my personal life had to do with one of my daughters, Kelsey. Although she's a fairly accomplished golfer, Kelsey had yet to receive any scholarship offers as of the middle of her junior year. Most kids receive offers during their senior year, but Kelsey wanted to put the recruiting process behind her as quickly as possible to enjoy her last year in high school.

I asked her to put together a list of her Top 10 most desired college programs, and she wrote a personalized letter to the head coach of each one. She requested an in-person meeting, which is considered an unofficial visit in that we would pay for the trip ourselves. I personally attended each of the visits with her, after having asked her to give me a certain cue if during the conversation she determined that this was the right school for her. Then I could jump in and help steer the conversation, or in other words, use the method!

In the middle of one of her visits, she gave me the magic cue, and I hopped in to help. At the time, her game was not quite at the level of most of the current players on the collegiate team, but I knew how hard she was working and I also knew that by the time she was a freshman in college she would be at least as good as the other players on the team.

After applying the method during the visit, Kelsey left with a scholarship offer in hand and will be attending her desired school next fall to begin her college golf career. To be clear, she 100 percent earned the scholarship on her own merits. At the same time, however, the use of the method was a very valuable tool in getting an offer under her desired timeline as opposed to waiting months for an answer.

When you're acting with integrity, honesty and trust, all the interactions in your life will benefit from your use of the Fuess Method.

CONCLUSION

We're all in sales even if we don't think we are. In fact, life is a series of mini-sales or even one long perpetual sale. In other words, we're influencing everyone around us at all times — whether we realize it or not.

At the core of the Fuess Method is the induction of action — action which is useful and purposeful. Most people fully recognize when they're being sold, but as I've explained, the beauty of the Fuess Method is that the people are selling themselves. The user or the method is, in essence, a traffic cop ensuring that traffic continues to move in the proper direction.

You might be thinking, "What are you talking about? I'm not selling anything. I'm just being myself!"

That's a normal response. But you are selling something all the time whether or not you're conscious of it.

For example, you're selling your spouse or your significant other on the truth that you care about them. Naturally, that's a positive thing. You want your loved ones to know you have their best interests in mind. You're selling them on that all the time. Of course, this isn't a game, and what you're demonstrating is how you truly feel about them.

The same thing goes for your children. You sell your children the concept of right and wrong, the concept that Mom and Dad love them, the concept that they are safe and you will be there to help them. You present the concept that when it's time to learn the tough lessons, you're going to let them learn, and when it's time to swoop in and save them, you're going to be right there. You sell your kids on the concept of trust and love and other things of that nature.

You sell your neighbors on the fact that they're great neighbors. You sell your friends that they're loyal and true friends. And then once you walk into your workplace, you're selling all day long to others — they're great co-workers, teammates, colleagues, employees, bosses, assistants. They're reliable; they're trustworthy; they're smart; they can get the job done. The list is endless.

I'd challenge you to think of a single occasion where you aren't selling. You can't do it!

Why not?

Because if you have relationships, then you're selling; communication within relationships is selling, plain and simple.

To everyone you communicate with, you're selling your viewpoints, your feelings, your desires, your beliefs and your history.

There are many authors out there who have written books on what effective communication and ineffective communication look like, but I would like you to understand that the very act of communicating is selling.

Let me give you an example. Let's take your relationship with your spouse or your children. You might think, "I'm not selling them. We're family, and they know I love and care for them."

"No, you're still actually selling your spouse and children all the time."

"What do you mean by that?"

"You're communicating, aren't you?"

"Well, sure but…"

"Imagine if you just came home after work, sat on the couch and refused to speak. Or went straight to the guest bedroom, shut and locked the door, and didn't come out for the rest of the evening."

"I would never do that!"

"Why not?"

"Because they might feel like I was angry, or I didn't care."

EXACTLY!

Your daily interactions — and all of your communications — are consistently and continually selling your family members on the idea that you still care about them as much as ever. You must sell them the idea that you always put their interests ahead of your own. Their comfort and feelings of security are essential for you to uphold continually. Refusing to speak to them would erode those beliefs in a heartbeat.

If you're using the Fuess Method in your daily life, it's not imperative to say anything specific like, "I still love you." Your loved ones feel it. In fact, it's much more effective if they just feel it. For the Fuess Method to work in the office, on a sales call, at the neighborhood HOA meeting, in your family, and when dealing with friends, you have to be genuine to start with. It has to be real.

In conclusion, if you have any relationships at all, then you're selling every time you communicate. Knowing that people like to buy from themselves and that people like to fall in love with their own ideas is key. Once you understand that you're always selling, you can take my conceptualized method for effectively selling across the entire gamut of life's experiences relationally and soar above the competition.

So why not recognize these interactions for what they are and become skillful at persuasion by using an artistic approach which is both ethical and moral, *and* highly effective?

Life, like sales, is a never-ending cycle of opportunities.

ACKNOWLEDGMENTS

Granddaddy — for inspiring me to be the best at whatever it is I choose to do

Dad — for teaching me his engineering-like ability to break big things down into small, manageable pieces

Mom — for passing along her 'people smarts'

All of the great sales leaders and managers I've had the opportunity to work with over the past 30 years

My team at Catapult — for being live guinea pigs while refining this approach

ABOUT THE AUTHORS

DAVID FUESS

As Chief Executive Officer for Catapult Systems, David's priorities include accelerating the growth and expansion of Catapult's business to new U.S. and global markets. He also sets the vision and strategy for the organization, fosters Catapult's strong relationship with its business partners, and continues refining the company's business model to provide a broader range and greater value of services and solutions.

David brings 25 years of leadership and management experience, including 18 years of experience in the IT professional services industry. David has organically started three offices for Catapult Systems, including the Dallas, Denver and Phoenix business units, while serving as Group Vice President and President. Prior to Catapult, David was the Dallas General Manager for BORN and previous to BORN, he served in the role of National Director of Sales for Avanade. David recently featured as a contributor to *Supreme Leadership* by bestselling author Alinka Rutkowska.

David studied business management at the University of Tulsa, graduating with honors in 1989. He was an All-American football player and record holder, and played in the Blue-Gray Football Classic all-star game in 1989. He lives in Austin, Texas and has two teenaged daughters, and his hobbies include golf, biking, hunting and pretty much anything outdoors. David is a former member of a Vistage CEO Peer Group in Colorado and previously sat on the Associate Board of Boys and Girls Clubs of Denver.

APOLLO GONZALEZ

Apollo Gonzalez serves as Chief Technology Officer for Catapult Systems. As Chief Technology Officer, he's responsible for driving innovation by transforming existing and emerging technologies into new service offerings for our clients, helping organizations validate or create actionable IT and business strategy roadmaps, mentoring and educating consultants and sales on emerging technologies, as well as connecting technology offerings and readiness with sales and marketing initiatives.

Apollo brings over 13 years of technology leadership and management experience, including 10 years of providing and delivering strategic solution to organizations. Apollo started as a Solution Architect for Catapult and quickly worked his way to CTO. Prior to Catapult, Apollo was the Director and Chief Technical Architect for Bernard Hodes Group.

Apollo studied hospitality management at the University of Houston, graduating with honors in 1999. He's a part-time professor at the University of Houston, lecturing in the Bauer College of Business about social business and cloud computing. Apollo lives in Fulshear, Texas with his wife and two children and loves reading, technology, basketball and spending as much time with family as possible.

RECOMMENDED READING

Armstrong, David, *Managing by Storying Around: a new method of leadership* (1992)

Dixon, Matthew and Adamson, Brent, *The Challenger Sale: taking control of the customer conversation* (2011)

Harding, Ford, *Creating Rainmakers: the manager's guide to training professionals to attract new clients* (2006)

Khalsa, Mahan, *Let's Get Real or Let's Not Play* (1999)

Maister, David H. and Green, Charles H. and Galford, Robert M., *The Trusted Advisor* (2000)

Mellon, Nancy, *The Art of Storytelling* (1998)

Miller, Robert B. and Heiman, Stephen E., *The New Conceptual Selling: the most effective and proven method for face-to-face sales planning* (2004)

Miller, Robert B. and Heiman, Stephen E., *The New Strategic Selling: the unique sales system proven successful by the world's best companies* (1998)

Rackham, Neil, *SPIN Selling: situation problem implication need-payoff* (1988)

Wood, J.B., Hewlin, Todd and Lah, Thomas, *Consumption Economics: the new rules of tech* (2011)

FREE BOOKLET!

Are you ready to realize the full potential of digitization in your business?

Ready to get more done, enhance your company culture, support your employees' productivity, and ensure your customers' data is safe and secure?

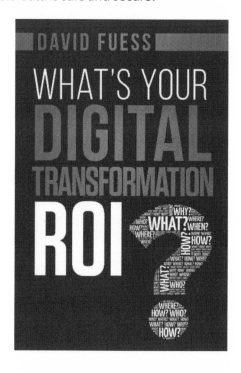

Go to https://get.catapultsystems.com/freebie/ and download a free copy of *What's Your Digital Transformation ROI?* to discover the digital transformation your business is missing.

Made in the USA
Middletown, DE
26 April 2019